Summary

TOOLS AND TECHNOLOGIES FOR AI.............................. 78

PRACTICAL APPLICATIONS OF AI 90

Introduction to Artificial Intelligence

What is Artificial Intelligence?

Artificial Intelligence (AI) is a field of computer science that focuses on developing systems and machines capable of performing tasks that normally require human intelligence. These tasks include learning, problem-solving, pattern recognition, natural language understanding, and decision-making.

AI can be defined as the simulation of human intelligence processes by machines, especially computer systems. These processes include:

- Learning (acquiring information and rules for using that information)
- Reasoning (using rules to reach approximate or definitive conclusions)
- Self-correction (ability to adjust and improve performance based on past experiences)

History of AI: from its origins to the present day

The history of AI, despite having a boom in recent years, its concept and study began more than 70 years ago.

- 1950s: The term "Artificial Intelligence" was coined by John McCarthy in 1956.
- 1960s-70s: First expert systems and development of programming languages for AI.
- 1980s-90s: Advances in machine learning and neural networks.

- 2000s-present: Big data explosion [1], increased computing power, and development of advanced deep learning techniques.

Difference between AI, Machine Learning and Deep Learning

Artificial intelligence

Artificial Intelligence is the broadest and most comprehensive concept of the three where AI refers to the creation of systems or machines capable of performing tasks that normally require human intelligence.

Features:

- It is a vast field that encompasses several subareas and techniques.
- Includes any technique that allows computers to imitate intelligent human behavior.
- It can be based on predefined rules or learning from data.

Examples:

- Expert systems
- Robotics
- Natural Language Processing
- Computer vision

---

[1] *Big Data refers to large volumes of structured and unstructured data that are processed and analyzed to extract valuable insights. It involves three main characteristics: volume, variety, and velocity.*

Machine Learning

Machine Learning is a subset of Artificial Intelligence that allows systems to automatically learn and improve from experience, without being explicitly programmed for each task.

Features:

- Focuses on creating algorithms that can learn from and make predictions or decisions based on data.
- Uses statistical methods to allow machines to "learn" from data.
- Requires less human intervention as models learn and adapt.

Main types:

- Supervised learning
- Unsupervised learning
- Reinforcement learning

Examples:

- Recommendation algorithms (like those used by Netflix or Amazon)
- Spam detection in emails
- Stock Price Prediction

Deep Learning

Deep Learning is a specialized subset of Machine Learning and is a Machine Learning technique based on artificial neural networks with multiple layers (hence the term "deep").

Features:

- Inspired by the structure and function of the human brain.

- It uses artificial neural networks with many layers (hidden layers) between input and output.
- Able to learn data representations with multiple levels of abstraction.
- It usually requires large amounts of data and significant computing power.

Advantages:

- Highly effective at complex tasks like image and speech recognition.
- Can discover intricate patterns in large data sets.

Examples:

- Advanced facial recognition
- Automatic language translation
- Self-driving cars
- Medical diagnosis from images

Main differences between the concepts:

Scope:

- AI is the broadest concept, encompassing any technique that allows machines to imitate human intelligence.
- Machine Learning is a subset of AI focused on algorithms that learn from data.
- Deep Learning is a specific Machine Learning technique using complex neural networks.

Human intervention:

- Traditional AI can rely heavily on human-programmed rules.

- Machine Learning reduces the need for human intervention as algorithms learn from data.
- Deep Learning requires even less human intervention in feature engineering, as neural networks can learn features automatically.

Complexity and computational power:

- AI varies in complexity.
- Machine learning generally requires more computing power than traditional rule-based AI.
- Deep Learning typically requires large amounts of data and significant computing power.

Applications:

- AI has a wide range of applications, from simple to complex systems.
- Machine Learning is particularly effective in classification, regression, and clustering problems.
- Deep Learning excels at complex tasks like image recognition, natural language processing, and gaming.

AI in everyday life: practical applications

Artificial Intelligence (AI) is revolutionizing virtually every aspect of our lives and industries. From everyday applications to complex solutions to global challenges, AI is proving to be a powerful and versatile tool. In this article, we will explore the diverse applications of AI across different industries, providing real-world examples of how this technology is being used to transform the world around us.

Health and Medicine

AI is having a significant impact on the healthcare industry, improving diagnostics, treatments, and the overall efficiency of medical care.

- **Imaging:** Google's DeepMind has developed an AI system that can detect breast cancer in mammograms with greater accuracy than human radiologists. In tests, the system reduced false positives by 5.7% and false negatives by 9.4%.
- **Drug Discovery:** Atomwise uses AI to accelerate the drug discovery process. Its AtomNet technology has analyzed millions of molecules and identified potential compounds to treat Ebola, reducing research time from years to just days.
- **Surgical Assistance:** The AI-assisted da Vinci robotic system is being used in hospitals around the world to perform minimally invasive surgeries with greater precision. In 2021, more than 1.2 million procedures were performed globally using this system.

Finance and Banking

The financial sector is adopting AI to improve security, efficiency and personalization of services.

- **Fraud Detection:** PayPal uses AI to combat financial fraud. Its machine learning system analyzes millions of transactions in real time, reducing the fraud rate to just 0.32% of payment volume.
- **Algorithmic Trading:** Two Sigma, a quantitative investment firm, uses AI and machine learning to analyze large volumes

of data and make investment decisions. As of 2020, the firm managed over $60 billion in assets.

- **Customer Service:** Bank of America launched Erica, an AI-powered virtual assistant that has assisted more than 17 million customers since its launch in 2018, answering queries and providing personalized financial guidance.

Transport and Logistics

AI is revolutionizing the way we move and how goods are transported.

- **Autonomous Vehicles:** Waymo, a subsidiary of Alphabet, has been testing self-driving cars on public roads. As of 2021, its vehicles had driven more than 20 million miles in autonomous mode, with plans to expand to more cities.
- **Route Optimization:** UPS uses the AI-based On-Road Integrated Optimization and Navigation (ORION) system to optimize delivery routes. This system saves approximately 10 million gallons of fuel annually and reduces 100,000 metric tons of CO_2 emissions.
- **Predictive Maintenance:** Lufthansa uses AI to predict aircraft equipment failures before they occur. This enables proactive maintenance, reducing flight delays and cancellations, and saving millions in maintenance costs.

Education

AI is transforming the education sector, offering more personalized and efficient learning experiences.

- **Personalized Tutoring:** CENTURY Tech, an adaptive learning platform, uses AI to create personalized study plans for each student. The platform analyzes student performance and adapts content in real-time, improving learning outcomes by up to 30%.

- **Automated Grading:** Gradescope, acquired by Turnitin, uses AI to grade and provide feedback on written assignments and exams. The platform is used by over 1,000 educational institutions and has reduced grading time by up to 70%.

- **Educational Accessibility:** Microsoft has developed Seeing AI, an application that uses AI to help people with visual impairments "see" the world around them. In education, this enables students with visual impairments to read text, recognize objects, and navigate educational environments with greater independence.

Manufacturing and Industry

AI is driving the fourth industrial revolution, known as Industry 4.0.

- **Quality Control:** NVIDIA has developed an AI-based visual inspection system that is used by manufacturers like BMW to detect defects in automotive components with 99% accuracy, significantly outperforming traditional methods.

- **Advanced Robotics:** Fanuc has collaborated with NVIDIA to create AI-enabled industrial robots that can learn new tasks through demonstration and imitation, reducing programming time from weeks to hours.

- **Supply Chain Management:** Siemens uses AI in its MindSphere platform to optimize industrial supply chains. The system predicts bottlenecks, optimizes inventories and reduces downtime, resulting in savings of millions of euros annually.

Agriculture and Environment

AI being applied to address environmental challenges and improve agricultural efficiency.

- **Precision Agriculture:** Startup Blue River Technology (acquired by John Deere) has developed AI-powered farm machinery that can identify and spray only weeds, reducing herbicide use by up to 90%.
- **Environmental Monitoring:** Conservation Metrics uses AI to analyze satellite imagery and acoustic recordings to monitor wildlife populations. Its system has helped track the recovery of blue whales in Antarctica and protect endangered species around the world.
- **Natural Disaster Prediction** : Google has developed an AI system to predict floods up to 48 hours in advance. The system is being used in India and Bangladesh, helping protect millions of people in flood-prone areas.

Entertainment and Media

AI is transforming the way content is created, distributed and consumed.

- **Content Recommendation:** Netflix's AI-powered recommendation algorithm powers 80% of the content watched on the platform. This personalized system saves the company approximately $1 billion per year in customer retention.
- **Content Creation:** OpenAI has developed GPT-3, an advanced language model that can generate text that is nearly indistinguishable from human-written text.

Companies like The Guardian have used GPT-3 to create opinion pieces.

- **Visual Effects:** Weta Digital, known for its work on films such as "The Lord of the Rings," uses AI to create realistic visual effects. Its technology has been used to create convincing digital characters in films such as "War for the Planet of the Apes."

Security and Surveillance

AI being applied to improve public and private security.

Facial Recognition: Dubai Airport has implemented a "smart tunnel" system that uses AI-based facial recognition to verify passengers' identities, reducing immigration clearance times to just 15 seconds.

Cyber Threat Detection: Cybersecurity company Darktrace uses AI to detect and respond to cyber threats in real time. Its Enterprise Immune System protects over 5,000 organizations globally against advanced cyberattacks.

Crime Prevention: The LAPD uses PredPol, an AI-based predictive policing software, to predict where and when crimes are most likely to occur, allowing for more efficient allocation of police resources.

Myths and truths about AI

Artificial Intelligence (AI) has been a topic of great interest and debate over the past few decades. As this technology advances rapidly, many myths and misconceptions have emerged around it. In this article, we will explore some of the most common myths about AI and contrast them with truths based on current facts and research.

Myth 1: AI will replace all human jobs

- **Myth:** Many people fear that AI will eventually replace all human jobs, leading to mass unemployment.
- **Truth:** While AI is certainly changing the employment landscape, it is more likely to transform jobs than eliminate them entirely. In fact, AI is creating new job opportunities and increasing productivity in many industries.

A study by the World Economic Forum predicts that while 85 million jobs could be displaced by AI by 2025, 97 million new roles could emerge.

AI is being used to automate repetitive tasks, allowing humans to focus on more creative and strategic work.

Myth 2: AI is completely objective and impartial

- **Myth:** Many believe that because it is based on data and algorithms, AI is inherently objective and free from bias.

- **Truth:** AI can, in fact, perpetuate and even amplify existing biases if not carefully designed and trained.

AI algorithms are trained on human-generated data, which may contain implicit biases.

Example: In 2018, Amazon discontinued an AI-powered recruiting tool because it was discriminating against female candidates, a reflection of the company's historical hiring patterns.

Myth 3: AI will soon surpass human intelligence in every aspect

- **Myth:** There is a popular belief that AI will soon catch up with and surpass human intelligence in all areas, a concept known as the "singularity."
- **Truth:** While AI has outperformed humans at specific tasks, human-level general intelligence is still far from being achieved.

Current AI is mostly "narrow" or specialized, excelling at specific tasks but lacking the versatility of human cognition.

Example: While DeepMind's AlphaGo defeated world champions at the game of Go, the same system cannot perform simple everyday tasks that a child can do.

Myth 4: AI does not require human intervention once implemented

- **Myth:** Once an AI system is developed and implemented, it can operate indefinitely without human supervision or intervention.
- **Truth:** AI systems require ongoing maintenance, updating, and oversight to remain effective and safe.

AI models need to be regularly retrained with new data to maintain their accuracy.

Human oversight is crucial to ensure that AI systems are working as intended and do not develop unwanted behaviors.

Myth 5: AI can explain all your decisions

- **Myth:** All AI systems can provide clear and understandable explanations for their decisions and actions.

- **Truth:** Many advanced AI systems, especially those based on deep learning, operate as "black boxes," making it difficult to explain exactly how they arrived at a particular decision.

This problem, known as "AI explainability," is an active area of research.

Example: In critical applications such as medical diagnostics, lack of explainability can be a significant barrier to widespread adoption of AI.

Myth 6: AI is infallible and always makes the best decisions

- **Myth:** Because AI systems are based on data analysis and complex algorithms, many believe they are infallible and always make the best decisions.
- **Truth:** AI systems can make mistakes and their decisions can be influenced by the quality of their training data and the way they were programmed.

AI is a powerful tool, but it is not perfect and still requires human oversight and validation.

Example: In 2020, an AI system used to predict exam grades in the UK yielded controversial results, leading to protests and eventually a reversal of AI-based decisions.

Truth 1: AI is rapidly improving at specific tasks

One undeniable truth about AI is that it is progressing rapidly in specific domains, often surpassing human performance.

In image recognition, medical diagnostics and complex games, AI has demonstrated impressive capabilities.

Example: DeepMind's AI system AlphaFold has made significant advances in predicting protein structure, a problem that has challenged scientists for decades.

Truth 2: AI is transforming entire industries

AI is having a transformative impact on virtually every sector of the economy. From manufacturing to healthcare, AI is being used to increase efficiency, reduce costs, and improve outcomes.

Example: In agriculture, AI systems are being used to optimize the use of water and pesticides, increasing productivity and reducing environmental impact.

Truth 3: Ethical considerations are crucial in AI development

As AI becomes more advanced and widespread, ethical questions surrounding its development and use are gaining greater importance.

Concerns about privacy, liability, and the social impact of AI are driving discussions about regulation and ethical guidelines.

Example: The European Union is developing comprehensive AI regulations to ensure that AI systems are safe, transparent, and respect fundamental rights.

In conclusion, Artificial Intelligence is a complex and rapidly evolving field surrounded by myths and misconceptions. While AI has the potential to dramatically transform our society and economy, it is important to approach both its capabilities and limitations with a realistic and fact-based understanding.

As we continue to develop and deploy AI systems, it is crucial to maintain an open and informed dialogue about their impacts. This includes addressing ethical concerns, working to mitigate bias, and ensuring that AI development benefits society as a whole.

The truth about AI is that it is a powerful tool with immense potential, but it also requires careful consideration and management. By separating the myths from the truths, we can better leverage the benefits of AI while navigating the challenges it presents.

Fundamental Concepts of AI

Artificial Intelligence (AI) is a field of computer science that aims to create systems capable of performing tasks that normally require human intelligence. These systems are designed to learn, reason, perceive, and interact with the environment in ways that simulate intelligent behavior. To understand AI, it is essential to understand its fundamental concepts.

These fundamental concepts form the basis of modern Artificial Intelligence. Understanding them is essential to appreciating the potential and challenges of AI. As technology continues to evolve, these concepts will intertwine in increasingly complex ways, leading to innovative applications in virtually every field of science and industry.

AI is not just a technology, but a multidisciplinary field that combines elements of computer science, mathematics, psychology, linguistics, and many other disciplines. Its impact continues to grow, transforming the way we live, work, and interact with the world around us.

AI Algorithms and Models

Machine Learning

Machine Learning is a subset of AI that focuses on algorithms that can learn and improve from data, without being explicitly programmed for each task.

Supervised Learning

In this type of learning, the model is trained on a labeled dataset where the desired inputs and outputs are known.

Main Algorithms:

- **Linear Regression:** Used to predict continuous values where an example use case is predicting property prices based on characteristics such as size and location.
- **Logistic Regression:** Used for binary classification, for example to predict whether an email is spam or not.
- **Decision Trees:** Models that make decisions based on a series of conditions that can be used for symptom-based medical diagnosis.
- **Random Forest:** A set of decision trees that work together to make predictions, used for example to predict credit risk in financial institutions.
- **Support Vector Machines (SVM):** Effective for classification and regression in high-dimensional spaces, where for example it is used for handwriting recognition.

Unsupervised Learning

These algorithms work with unlabeled data, seeking to find patterns or structures in the data.

Main Algorithms:

- **K-Means Clustering:** Groups data into K clusters based on similarity where it can be used for customer segmentation in marketing.
- **Hierarchical Clustering:** Creates a hierarchy of clusters to use for example in genomic data analysis.
- **Principal Component Analysis (PCA):** Reduces the dimensionality of data while preserving variance which is used for image compression and noise reduction.

- **Association Analysis:** Discovers relationships between variables in large data sets, where it is used for example in shopping basket analysis in e-commerce.

Reinforcement Learning

This type of learning involves an agent learning to make decisions by interacting with an environment, receiving rewards or penalties.

Main Algorithms:

- **Q-Learning:** Learns an optimal action policy for any [2]finite Markovian decision process, where it is used in strategy games, robotics.
- **SARSA (State-Action-Reward-State-Action):** Similar to Q-Learning, but considers the current policy when updating values, which is used for robot control in dynamic environments.
- **Deep Q-Network (DQN):** Combines Q-Learning with deep neural networks, which is used for example in Atari games, where the agent learns directly from the pixels on the screen, becoming a great player.

Neural Networks and Deep Learning

Neural networks are models inspired by the functioning of the human brain, composed of layers of interconnected "neurons". Deep Learning refers to neural networks with multiple hidden layers.

---

[2]*Markovian is a stochastic process where the probability of a future event depends only on the current state, without considering past events. It is based on the Markov property, known as "no memory".*

Feedforward Neural Networks

The simplest form of neural network, where information flows in one direction.

- **Perceptron:** The most basic type of neural network, capable of linear binary classification, where it is used for simple classification, such as determining whether a point is above or below a line.
- **Multilayer Perceptron (MLP):** Networks with one or more hidden layers, capable of learning non-linear representations used for example for handwritten digit recognition.

Convolutional Neural Networks (CNNs)

Especially effective for processing data with a grid structure, such as images used for facial recognition, object detection, image classification. For example, the ResNet-152 network achieved higher than human accuracy in classifying images from ImageNet.

Recurrent Neural Networks (RNNs)

Designed to work with sequences of data, maintaining an internal state.

- **Long Short-Term Memory (LSTM):** A type of RNN capable of learning long-term dependencies used for machine translation, text generation.
- **Gated Recurrent Unit (GRU):** Similar to LSTM, but with a simpler structure, used for example for time series analysis, stock forecasting.

Transformers

An architecture based on attention mechanisms, which revolutionized natural language processing where it can be used for automatic translation, text summarization, language generation where for example OpenAI's GPT (Generative Pre-trained Transformer) model is capable of generating coherent and contextually relevant text.

Generative Adversarial Networks (GANs)

They consist of two competing models: a generator and a discriminator that can be applied to realistic image generation, data augmentation, and style transfer.

NVIDIA's StyleGAN can generate photorealistic human faces that don't exist.

Optimization Algorithms

Essential for training AI models, especially deep neural networks.

- **Gradient Descent:** The most basic optimization algorithm, which adjusts model parameters in the opposite direction to the gradient of the loss function.
- **Stochastic Gradient Descent (SGD):** A variation of Gradient Descent that uses random subsets of the training data at each iteration.
- **Adam (Adaptive Moment Estimation):** Combines the advantages of two other optimization algorithms: AdaGrad and RMSProp.

Search and Planning Algorithms

Used in AI to find optimal solutions in complex problem spaces.

- **A* Search:** An informed search algorithm that finds the least cost path between two points used in game navigation, route planning.
- **Minimax:** A decision-making algorithm for two-player zero-sum games, where it is an AI for the board games of chess and Go.
- **Monte Carlo Tree Search (MCTS):** A heuristic search method for some types of decision processes that is used in AI for complex games, planning in robotics.

Natural Language Processing (NLP)

Specific algorithms and models for working with human language.

- **Word Embeddings:** Vector representations of words that capture semantic relationships, such as the tools Word2Vec, GloVe, FastText.
- **Sequence-to-Sequence Models:** Used for tasks that involve transforming one sequence into another used in machine translation, text summarization.
- **BERT (Bidirectional Encoder Representations from Transformers):** A pre-trained language model that has revolutionized several NLP tasks that can be applied in text classification, question answering, sentiment analysis.

Computer Vision

Algorithms and models for image and video processing and analysis.

- **YOLO (You Only Look Once):** A real-time object detection algorithm that is used in surveillance systems, self-driving cars.
- **U-Net:** A network architecture for biomedical image segmentation, where its application is made for tumor analysis in magnetic resonance imaging.

Conclusion

AI algorithms and models form a vast and constantly evolving ecosystem. Each type of algorithm or model has its own strengths and weaknesses, and is best suited for certain types of problems and data. Choosing the right algorithm or model depends on the specific nature of the problem, the quantity and quality of the data available, and the computing resources available.

As the field of AI continues to advance, new algorithms and models are constantly being developed, expanding the capabilities and applications of AI. The current trend is toward more complex and larger-scale models, such as large language models and multimodal models that can process different types of data simultaneously.

Machine Learning: The Heart of AI

Machine learning is truly the beating heart of modern artificial intelligence (AI). This revolutionary field of computer science enables AI systems to evolve and adapt autonomously, without being explicitly programmed for each specific task. Just as the heart pumps life throughout the human body, machine learning infuses life and adaptability into AI systems by allowing them to learn from data and experience, continually improving their performance over time.

Machine learning's essence lies in its ability to discover patterns in large volumes of data and use those insights to make predictions or decisions. This ability is analogous to the way the human heart responds to the body's needs, adjusting its rhythm and pumping force as needed. Similarly, machine learning algorithms adjust their internal parameters as they are exposed to more data, constantly refining their understanding and responsiveness. This adaptability makes machine learning fundamental to a wide range of AI applications, from virtual assistants and recommendation systems to medical diagnostics and autonomous vehicles.

Just as the heart has different chambers and valves working in harmony, machine learning encompasses a variety of techniques and approaches. These include supervised learning, where the model is trained on labeled data; unsupervised learning, which discovers patterns in unlabeled data; and reinforcement learning, where models learn through interactions with an environment. Each of these approaches plays a crucial role in enabling AI to approach different types of problems and adapt to different scenarios, just as the heart adapts to the different demands of the body.

Ultimately, just as a healthy heart is essential to an organism's overall well-being, well-implemented machine learning is crucial to the success and effectiveness of AI systems. It provides the capacity for continuous learning and adaptation that distinguishes truly intelligent AI from simple rule-based systems. As the field evolves, with advances like deep learning and increasingly sophisticated models, machine learning continues to push the boundaries of what is possible in AI, driving innovations that are transforming entire industries and societies. Thus, machine learning is not only the heart of AI, but also the engine that drives its continued progress and transformative impact on the world.

How Machine Learning Models Work

Machine learning (ML) models are computer systems designed to learn from data, identify patterns, and make decisions with minimal human intervention. These models are the foundation of modern artificial intelligence and have applications in everything from image recognition to financial forecasting. Let's explore how these models work, from their inception to their practical applications.

Data Collection and Preparation

The first crucial step in running any ML model is data collection and preparation.

- **Data Collection:** Data can come from a variety of sources, such as databases, sensors, or manual input.
- **Data Cleaning:** Involves removing inconsistent data, handling missing values, and correcting errors.
- **Normalization:** Adjusts data values to a common scale, making it easier for the model to process.
- **Data Splitting:** Generally, data is split into training, validation, and testing sets.

Model Selection

The selection of the appropriate model depends on the nature of the problem and the data available.

- **Regression Models:** To predict continuous values.
- **Classification Models:** To categorize data into discrete classes.
- **Clustering Models:** To group similar data.
- **Neural Networks:** For complex problems that require deep learning.

Model Training

This is the phase where the model "learns" from the data.

- **Initialization:** The model starts with random or predefined parameters.
- **Data Feeding:** Training data is fed to the model.
- **Forward Pass:** The model makes predictions based on the input data.
- **Error Calculation:** The difference between the model predictions and the actual values is calculated.
- **Backward Pass:** The error is propagated back through the model.
- **Parameter Tuning:** Model parameters are tuned to minimize error.
- **Iteration:** This process is repeated many times, with the model gradually improving.
-

Cost Function and Optimization

The cost function measures how well the model is performing.

- **Defining the Cost Function:** An appropriate metric, such as mean squared error, is chosen.

- **Optimization:** Algorithms like Gradient Descent are used to minimize the cost function.

Regularization

Techniques to prevent overfitting (when the model fits too much to the training data).

- **L1/L2 Regularization:** Adds penalties to model parameters.
- **Dropout:** Randomly disables neurons during training (in neural networks).
- **Early Stopping:** Stops training when performance on the validation set stops improving.

Validation

The validation set is used to tune hyperparameters and avoid overfitting.

- **Cross-Validation:** Technique to evaluate the model's performance on different subsets of the data.

Testing and Evaluation

The model is tested on data it has never seen before to assess its actual performance.

- **Evaluation Metrics:** Depending on the problem, these may include accuracy, precision, recall, F1-score, etc.

Inference and Deployment

Once trained and validated, the model can be used to make predictions on new data.

- **Deployment:** The model is integrated into production systems.
- **Monitoring:** Model performance is continuously monitored.
- **Update:** The model can be retrained periodically with new data.

Practical Example: Email Classification

Let's consider an ML model to classify emails as spam or not spam:

- **Data Collection:** Thousands of emails labeled as spam or not spam are collected.
- **Preparation:** Emails are converted into feature vectors (e.g. frequency of certain words).
- **Model Choice:** A classifier, such as Support Vector Machine (SVM), is chosen.
- **Training:** The SVM learns to separate spam emails from non-spam emails based on features.
- **Validation:** The model is tested on a separate set of emails to tune hyperparameters.
- **Testing:** Final performance is evaluated on an independent test set.
- **Deployment:** The model is integrated into the email system to classify new messages in real time.

Conclusion

Machine learning models are a complex process that involves multiple steps, from data preparation to final deployment. The key to the success of these models lies in data quality, appropriate algorithm selection, and careful optimization and validation. As the field evolves, new techniques and approaches continue to emerge, expanding the capabilities and applications of machine learning across a variety of domains.

It's important to note that while the basic principles remain the same, different types of ML models may have specific characteristics and processes. For example, the workings of a deep neural network will be more complex than a simple linear regression model. However, understanding these fundamental principles provides a solid foundation for exploring and working with different types of Machine Learning models.

Types of algorithms: regression, classification, clustering[3]

Machine learning algorithms are traditionally categorized into three main groups: regression, classification, and clustering. Each type has its own set of characteristics, applications, and challenges. Let's explore each of them in detail.

Regression Algorithms

Regression is a type of supervised learning algorithm used to predict continuous numerical values. The goal is to establish a relationship between independent variables (features) and a continuous dependent variable.

Examples of Algorithms:

- Simple and Multiple Linear Regression

---

[3]Clustering is an unsupervised learning technique that groups similar data into clusters or groups. The goal is for elements within a group to be more similar to each other than to those in other groups.

- Polynomial Regression
- Ridge and Lasso Regression
- Decision Trees for Regression
- Random Forest for Regression

Uses:

- Real estate price prediction based on features such as size, location, etc.
- Estimating a company's future sales
- Temperature forecast based on climatic factors
- Analysis of the impact of advertising campaigns on sales

Positive Points:

- Easy to understand and interpret, especially linear regression
- Effective for modeling linear relationships between variables
- Can provide insights into the relative importance of different features
- Versatile, with variants capable of handling non-linear relationships

Negative Points:

- Assumes a linear relationship between variables (in the case of simple linear regression)
- Sensitive to outliers, which can distort results
- May perform poorly with highly non-linear relationships
- Risk of overfitting, especially with many features or in high-degree polynomial regression

Classification Algorithms

Classification is a type of supervised learning algorithm used to predict discrete categories or classes. The goal is to learn a model that assigns correct class labels to new, unseen examples.

Examples of Algorithms:

- Logistic Regression
- Decision Trees for Classification
- Random Forest for Classification
- Support Vector Machines (SVM)
- Naive Bayes
- K-Nearest Neighbors (KNN)

Uses:

- Spam detection in emails
- Medical diagnosis (e.g., classifying a tumor as benign or malignant)
- Handwritten digit recognition
- Forecast of default on bank loans
- Sentiment classification in text analysis

Positive Points:

- Effective for binary or multiclass decision problems
- Some algorithms (like decision trees) are easy to interpret
- Can handle non-linear relationships between features
- Variety of algorithms available for different types of data and problems

Negative Points:

- Some algorithms are prone to overfitting (such as very deep decision trees)

- May be sensitive to imbalances in the classes of the dataset
- Algorithms like SVM can be computationally intensive for large datasets
- Choosing the right algorithm can be challenging and depends heavily on the nature of the data.

Clustering Algorithms

Clustering is a type of unsupervised learning algorithm used to group unlabeled data into clusters or groups based on similarities. The goal is to discover intrinsic structures in the data.

Examples of Algorithms:

- K-Means
- Hierarchical Clustering
- DBSCAN (Density-Based Spatial Clustering of Applications with Noise)
- Gaussian Mixture Models
- Mean Shift Clustering

Uses:

- Customer segmentation in marketing
- Social network analysis to identify communities
- Grouping documents by similar topics
- Anomaly detection in security systems
- Gene expression analysis in bioinformatics

Positive Points:

- Does not require labeled data, making it useful when labels are expensive or impossible to obtain

- Useful for discovering hidden structures and patterns in data
- Can handle large volumes of data
- Flexible and applicable to a variety of domains

Negative Points:

- The choice of the number of clusters can be subjective (in algorithms like K-Means)
- Sensitive to initial choice of centroids or starting points (K-Means)
- May have difficulty with clusters of unconventional shapes or varying densities
- Interpreting the resulting clusters can be challenging and subjective

Comparison and Final Considerations of their uses

Nature of the Problem:

- Regression is ideal for predicting continuous values.
- Classification is best for categorizing into discrete classes.
- Clustering is useful for discovering natural groups in unlabeled data.

Type of Learning:

- Regression and Classification are forms of supervised learning, requiring labeled data.
- Clustering is a form of unsupervised learning, not requiring labels.

Interpretability:

- Algorithms like Linear Regression and Decision Trees tend to be more interpretable.
- More complex algorithms like Random Forest or SVM may be less transparent in their decisions.

Scalability:

- Some algorithms (such as K-Means for clustering) are efficient for large data sets.
- Others (like SVM for classification) may struggle with very large datasets.

Data Preparation:

- Regression usually requires feature normalization.
- Clustering can be sensitive to the scale of the features.
- Some classification algorithms (such as Naive Bayes) can handle categorical data well.

The choice between regression, classification, or clustering algorithms fundamentally depends on the nature of the problem, the characteristics of the available data, and the specific goals of the Machine Learning project. Each type of algorithm has its own strengths and weaknesses, and selecting the appropriate algorithm is a crucial part of the ML model development process.

It is common in practice to try out multiple algorithms for a given problem and compare their performance. Additionally, advanced techniques such as ensemble learning, which combines multiple algorithms, can be used to overcome the limitations of individual algorithms.

As the field of Machine Learning continues to evolve, new algorithms and variations are developed, further expanding the possibilities and applications of these techniques across diverse domains. A deep understanding of these fundamental types of algorithms provides a solid foundation for exploring and applying Machine Learning to a wide range of real-world problems.

Model training: data, features and adjustments

Machine learning model training is a crucial process that determines the effectiveness and accuracy of the final model. This process involves three main components: data, features, and tuning. Each of these elements plays a vital role in creating a robust and efficient model.

Data

Data is the foundation of any Machine Learning model. The quality and quantity of data available has a direct impact on the model's performance.

Data Collection

- **Data Sources:** Can include databases, APIs, web scraping, sensors, or manual input.
- **Volume:** Generally, the more data, the better. However, quality is just as important as quantity.
- **Diversity:** The data must be representative of the real problem that the model will try to solve.

Data Preparation

- **Cleansing:** Removing duplicate data, handling missing values, correcting errors.

- **Normalization/Standardization:** Adjusting values to a common scale to prevent features with larger scales from dominating the model.
- **Encoding:** Conversion of categorical data into numeric formats (e.g. one-hot encoding, label encoding).

Data Division

- **Training Set:** Used to train the model (usually 60-80% of the data).
- **Validation Set:** Used to tune hyperparameters and avoid overfitting (usually 10-20%).
- **Test Set:** Used to evaluate the final performance of the model (usually 10-20%).

Features

Features are the input variables used by the model to make predictions. Selecting and engineering appropriate features is critical to the success of the model.

Feature Selection

- **Relevance:** Choosing features that have a significant relationship with the target variable.
- **Correlation:** Identification and treatment of highly correlated features to avoid multicollinearity.
- **Selection Techniques** : These may include statistical methods such as Pearson correlation, or algorithms such as Lasso and Ridge Regression.

- **Creation of New Features:** Combination of existing features or creation of new ones based on domain knowledge.
- **Transformation:** Application of mathematical functions to capture non-linear relationships (e.g. logarithm, square root).
- **Binning:** Grouping continuous values into discrete categories.

Dimensionality Reduction

- **PCA (Principal Component Analysis):** Reduces dimensionality while maintaining maximum variance.
- **t-SNE:** Useful for visualizing high-dimensional data.
- **Autoencoders:** Neural networks that can be used for non-linear dimensionality reduction.

Settings

Tuning refers to the process of optimizing the model to improve its performance and generalization.

Hyperparameters

- **Definition:** Parameters that are not learned by the model during training, but are defined beforehand.
- **Examples:** Learning rate, number of trees in a Random Forest, number of layers in a neural network.
- **Optimization Techniques:** Grid Search, Random Search, Bayesian Optimization.

Regularization

- **Objective:** Prevent overfitting, improving model generalization.
- **Techniques:** L1 (Lasso), L2 (Ridge), Elastic Net, Dropout (for neural networks).

Cross-Validation

- **Purpose:** To evaluate the performance of the model on different subsets of the data.
- **Techniques:** K-Fold Cross-Validation, Stratified K-Fold, Leave-One-Out Cross-Validation.

Monitoring and Evaluation

- **Metrics:** Choosing appropriate metrics (e.g. accuracy, precision, recall, F1-score, RMSE).
- **Learning Curves:** Monitoring performance on training and validation sets over time.
- **Error Analysis:** Identifying patterns in model errors to guide improvements.

Fine-Tuning

- **Iteration:** Continuous process of adjustment based on evaluation results.
- **Ensemble Methods:** Combining multiple models to improve overall performance.

Training machine learning models is an iterative and often complex process. Data quality, appropriate feature selection and engineering, and careful tuning are all crucial to developing an effective model.

- **Balance:** It is important to find a balance between model complexity and generalizability. Models that are too simple can suffer from underfitting, while models that are too complex can lead to overfitting.

- **Interpretability vs. Performance** : Sometimes there is a trade-off [4]between model interpretability and performance. More complex models (like deep learning) may offer better performance, but are less interpretable.
- **Continuous Updates:** Model training is not a one-time process. As new data becomes available, models must be retrained and adjusted to maintain their accuracy and relevance.

- **Ethics and Bias:** It is crucial to be aware of potential biases in data and models, especially in applications that affect important decisions about people.
- **Documentation:** Maintaining clear documentation of all steps in the training process is essential for future reproducibility and maintenance.

Successfully training machine learning models requires a combination of technical knowledge, practical experience, and a deep understanding of the problem domain. As the field evolves, new techniques and tools continue to emerge, making model training a dynamic and ever-evolving field.

---

[4]*A trade-off is a situation in which two or more conflicting options must be balanced, where improving one characteristic may imply deteriorating another. It is a decision that involves concessions between benefits and costs.*

Model evaluation: accuracy, precision, recall and F1-score

Model evaluation is a crucial step in the machine learning process. It allows us to quantify the performance of a model and compare it to others. While there are several evaluation metrics, four of the most commonly used are accuracy, precision, recall, and F1-score. Each of these metrics provides different insights into model performance and is particularly useful in specific contexts.

Confusion Matrix

Before we dive into the individual metrics, it's important to understand the concept of a confusion matrix. A confusion matrix is a table that describes the performance of a classification model on a test dataset for which the true values are known.

For a binary classification problem, the confusion matrix has four elements:

- **True Positives (TP):** Cases correctly identified as positive
- **True Negatives (TN):** Cases correctly identified as negative
- **False Positives (FP):** Negative cases incorrectly identified as positive (Type I Error)
- **False Negatives (FN):** Positive cases incorrectly identified as negative (Type II Error)

Accuracy

Accuracy is the most intuitive and straightforward metric. It represents the proportion of correct predictions (both positive and negative) among the total number of cases examined.

Formula: Accuracy = (VP + VN) / (VP + VN + FP + FN)

When to use:

- Balanced datasets (similar number of samples in each class)
- When the costs of false positives and false negatives are similar

Limitations:

- Can be misleading in imbalanced datasets
- Does not provide information about the types of errors the model is making

Precision

Accuracy measures the proportion of positive identifications that were actually correct. In other words, of the total cases that the model identified as positive, how many were actually positive?

Formula: Accuracy = VP / (VP + FP)

When to use:

- When the cost of false positives is high
- In tasks such as spam filtering, where it is important not to misclassify legitimate emails as spam

Limitations:

- Does not consider false negatives
- A model that makes just one positive prediction and gets it right may be 100% accurate, but it is not necessarily useful.

Recall (Sensitivity)

Recall measures the proportion of true positives that were correctly identified. Of the total number of cases that are true positives, how many did the model identify correctly?

Formula: Recall = VP / (VP + FN)

When to use:

- When the cost of false negatives is high
- In medical diagnostics, where it is crucial not to miss positive cases of a disease

Limitations:

- Does not consider false positives
- A model that classifies everything as positive would have 100% recall, but would not be useful in practice

F1-Score

The F1-score is the harmonic mean between precision and recall, providing a single number that balances both metrics.

Formula: F1 = 2 * (Precision * Recall) / (Precision + Recall)

When to use:

- When you need a balance between precision and recall
- In imbalanced data sets
- When you want a single metric to compare models

Limitations:

- Does not differentiate between false positives and false negatives
- May obscure important details about model performance in specific cases

Choosing the Right Metric

Choosing the right evaluation metric depends on the specific context of the problem:

- **Accuracy:** Useful for balanced problems where all types of errors have similar costs.
- **Accuracy:** Prioritize when false positives are more costly or undesirable.
- **Recall:** Focus on when false negatives are most problematic or dangerous.
- **F1-Score:** Use when seeking a balance between precision and recall, especially on imbalanced datasets.

Additional Considerations

- **ROC curve and AUC:** For a more complete view of model performance at different classification thresholds.
- **Cross-Validation:** To assess how the model generalizes to independent data sets.
- **Domain-Specific Metrics:** Some areas have custom metrics that are more relevant to their specific problems.

Model evaluation is an essential part of the machine learning process. Accuracy, precision, recall, and F1-score are key metrics that provide different insights into model performance. The choice of the appropriate metric depends on the nature of the problem, the characteristics of the dataset, and the specific consequences of different types of errors in the context of the application.

It is important to remember that no single metric captures all aspects of a model's performance. A comprehensive evaluation usually involves consideration of multiple metrics as well as a qualitative analysis of model errors. Furthermore, the interpretation of these metrics should always be done in the context of the specific problem being addressed.

As the field of Machine Learning continues to evolve, new metrics and evaluation techniques are developed to address specific challenges and complex scenarios. Keeping up to date with these developments is crucial to ensuring accurate and meaningful evaluation of Machine Learning models.

Overfitting and underfitting

In the context of Machine Learning, the concepts of overfitting and underfitting are related to the performance of the model in relation to the training data set and the test set. Both are problems that can impact the generalization ability of the model and, consequently, its efficiency in making predictions on unseen data.

Overfitting

Overfitting occurs when a model is overfitted to the training data, capturing not only the true patterns but also the noise and irrelevant variance. As a result, the model performs exceptionally well on the training set but fails to generalize to new data.

Causes of Overfitting:

- Very complex model in relation to the volume of data available.
- Prolonged training without regularization techniques.
- Excess of irrelevant or redundant features.

How to avoid Overfitting:

- Use regularization (e.g. L1 and L2, Dropout in neural networks).
- Increase the amount of training data.
- Reduce model complexity.
- Apply cross-validation to evaluate model performance on different data subsets.

Underfitting

Underfitting occurs when the model is overly simple and fails to capture the underlying patterns in the data. This results in poor performance on both training and testing data, indicating that the model is not learning properly.

Causes of Underfitting:

- Model with insufficient capacity (example: a linear regression trying to capture a non-linear relationship).
- Too little training data.
- Inadequate use of features (lack of relevant variables).
- Insufficient training.

How to avoid Underfitting:

- Increase the complexity of the model (example: add layers to a neural network or use a more sophisticated model).
- Include more relevant features.
- Tune hyperparameters appropriately.
- Increase training time.

Finding Balance

The goal in Machine Learning is to find a model that falls between overfitting and underfitting, capturing relevant patterns without memorizing noise. This can be achieved through techniques such as cross-validation, hyperparameter tuning, and regularization.

The classic graph to illustrate this balance shows the relationship between training error and testing error:

- When the training error is very low but the testing error is high, it indicates overfitting.

- When both errors are high, there is underfitting.

- The sweet spot is where testing error is minimized without excessively low training error.

Avoiding overfitting and underfitting is a key challenge in developing machine learning models. The key to a successful model is finding the right balance between complexity and generalizability, ensuring that the model can learn the right patterns and apply them effectively to new data.

Deep Learning: Artificial Neural Networks

What are neural networks?

A neural network in Artificial Intelligence is a computational model inspired by the functioning of the human brain. Just as our brain is made up of billions of interconnected neurons that process information, an artificial neural network is made up of units called artificial neurons, organized in layers that work together to recognize patterns and make decisions.

Analogy with the Human Brain

We can imagine a neural network as a large group of workers organized into different sectors within a company:

- Each worker (neuron) is given a specific task.
- It processes the information and passes it on to another sector (next layer).
- The better trained the workers are, the more efficient the company will be.

In the case of neural networks, the "workers" adjust their connections based on the experience they gain (a process called training), making the network more accurate over time.

Structure of a Neural Network

A typical neural network has three main types of layers:

- **Input layer:** Receives the raw data (example: an image or text).
- **Hidden layers:** Process information and learn patterns through mathematical calculations.
- **Output layer:** Produces the final response of the model (example: identifying a cat in a photo or translating a text).

Practical Example: Digit Recognition

Imagine an application that recognizes handwritten numbers:

- The image of the number "8" is sent to the neural network.
- The neurons in the input layer receive the pixels from the image.
- The hidden layers analyze the number's features and try to find patterns that are similar to the learned numbers.
- The output layer says, "This number is an 8!"

Neural networks are the basis of many modern AI applications, such as facial recognition, virtual assistants, and self-driving cars. Thanks to their ability to learn from examples, they continue to evolve and improve their accuracy, making the technology increasingly powerful and present in our daily lives.

Popular architectures: CNNs, RNNs, GANs

Neural networks come in different architectures, each optimized for specific tasks. Some of the most popular include Convolutional Neural Networks (CNNs), Recurrent Neural Networks (RNNs), and Generative Adversarial Networks (GANs). The choice of architecture depends on the type of problem to be solved.

Each neural architecture has its advantages and is designed to solve specific problems. CNNs are ideal for images, RNNs specialize in sequential data, and GANs are powerful in generating new content. The appropriate choice of architecture depends on the type of data and the objective of the application, ensuring more efficient and accurate solutions in Artificial Intelligence.

Convolutional Neural Networks (CNNs)

CNNs (Convolutional Neural Networks) are designed to process data with spatial structure, such as images and videos. They use convolutional layers that automatically extract relevant features from the input data, reducing the need for manual preprocessing.

Application Example

- Facial recognition in photos and videos.
- Medical diagnosis through analysis of X-ray images.
- Object detection in autonomous vehicles.

Strengths

- Excellent for analyzing images and videos.
- They significantly reduce the need for feature engineering.
- Greater efficiency in processing large volumes of visual data.

Recurrent Neural Networks (RNNs)

RNNs (Recurrent Neural Networks) are designed to handle sequential data, where the order of the elements influences the interpretation. Unlike traditional networks, RNNs have recurrent connections that allow them to maintain an internal state, making them ideal for tasks involving temporal dependencies.

Application Example

- Natural language processing (machine translation, chatbots, automatic captioning).
- Time series analysis (demand forecasting, financial market analysis).

- Speech recognition and voice commands.

Strengths

- Capture temporal and contextual relationships in data.
- Ideal for natural language processing and time series analysis.
- Variants such as LSTMs and GRUs improve information retention over time.

Generative Adversarial Networks (GANs)

GANs (Generative Adversarial Networks) are architectures designed to generate new, realistic data. They consist of two neural models: a generator, which creates synthetic samples, and a discriminator, which evaluates whether the generated sample is real or fake. This iterative process results in the creation of extremely realistic data.

Application Example

- Realistic image generation for art and design.
- Creating deepfakes to simulate human faces.
- Increased datasets to train AI models with greater diversity.

Strengths

- Capable of generating new and realistic data.
- Applicable in areas such as art, entertainment and cybersecurity.
- Potential to improve models by expanding limited datasets.

Deep learning on images, videos and audios

Deep learning has revolutionized the way machines understand and process different types of data, such as images, videos, and audio. Using deep neural networks, these models can learn complex patterns and perform tasks previously considered exclusive to human intelligence.

Deep Learning on Images

Convolutional neural networks [5](CNNs) are widely used for image processing because they can automatically extract relevant features such as edges, textures, and shapes. These networks learn hierarchically, allowing them to recognize objects and faces with high accuracy.

Application Example

- Medical diagnosis through imaging tests (x-rays, magnetic resonance imaging).
- Facial recognition systems for user authentication.
- Object detection in autonomous vehicles.

Strengths

- High accuracy in visual pattern analysis.
- Reduced need for manual feature engineering.
- Ability to operate on images of different resolutions and formats.

---

[5]*Convolutional refers to convolutional neural networks (CNNs), which are deep learning models primarily used to process and analyze image data. They use convolutional layers to extract local features and detect spatial patterns.*

Deep Learning in Videos

To process videos, deep learning uses a combination of CNNs and Recurrent Neural Networks (RNNs), allowing analysis not only of the content of each frame, but also of the temporal sequence of the images. This makes it possible to understand actions and events in real time.

Application Example

- Intelligent surveillance systems to detect suspicious activities.
- Sports analytics to identify game patterns.
- Automatic generation of subtitles in videos.

Strengths

- Ability to process temporal sequences and identify movement patterns.
- Applications in security monitoring and entertainment.
- Improvements in video compression and quality through adaptive learning.

Deep Learning in Audio

Deep learning audio processing is performed by models such as Recurrent Neural Networks (RNNs) and Transformers, which can interpret sound signals, identify patterns and perform tasks such as speech recognition and voice synthesis.

Application Example

- Virtual assistants like Alexa, Google Assistant and Siri.
- Automatic translation of audio to text.
- Sentiment analysis in customer service calls.

Strengths

- Better understanding of spoken language and its contexts.
- Direct applications in accessibility and human-machine interaction.
- Ability to continuously improve with additional data.

Generative AI

What is Generative AI?

Generative Artificial Intelligence (AI) refers to a subset of machine learning techniques that enable AI systems to create new and original content, such as text, images, music, video, and even programming code. These AIs are capable of generating data that is similar, but not identical, to the data they were trained on.

Basic Operation

Generative AI works through a two main step process:

- **Training:** The model is fed with large amounts of existing data (e.g. text, images, sounds).
- **Generation:** After training, the model can create content based on the learned patterns.

Types of Generative AI

There are several types of generative AI, each specialized for different types of content:

- Language Models: Generate text (e.g. GPT-3, BERT)
- Generative Adversarial Networks (GANs): Create realistic images
- Variational Autoencoders (VAEs): Generate images and other types of data
- Diffusion Models: Create high quality images (e.g. DALL-E, Midjourney)
- Speech Synthesis Models: Generate Realistic Human Speech
- Music Composition Templates: Create Original Music

Generative AI Applications

The applications of generative AI are vast and ever-expanding:

- Content Creation: Writing articles, scripts, poems
- Design and Art: Creation of images, illustrations, layouts
- Product Development: Idea Generation and Prototyping
- Entertainment: Character creation, game scenarios
- Medicine: Generating synthetic medical images for training
- Education: Creating personalized teaching materials
- Scientific Research: Scenario simulation and hypothesis generation

Popular models: GPT, DALL-E, Stable Diffusion

Generative Artificial Intelligence has revolutionized several areas, from text creation to image generation. Three models stand out in this scenario: GPT, DALL-E and Stable Diffusion. Let's explore each of them in detail.

Each of these models—GPT, DALL-E, and Stable Diffusion—represents a significant advancement in generative AI, offering unique capabilities in generating text and images. While GPT excels at creating coherent, contextually relevant text, DALL-E and Stable Diffusion open up new frontiers in generating images from textual descriptions.

These models not only demonstrate the impressive potential of generative AI, but also raise important ethical and practical questions about the future of content creation, intellectual property, and AI's role in society. As these technologies continue to evolve, it is crucial to maintain a balance between innovation and responsibility, ensuring that their development and application are guided by ethical principles and societal benefits. Let's take a look at each of these in turn.

GPT (Generative Pre-trained Transformer)

GPT is a language model based on the Transformer architecture. It is trained on large volumes of text to predict the next word in a sequence, allowing it to generate coherent and contextually relevant text. It works in a few steps:

- **Pre-training:** The model is exposed to billions of words of diverse text.
- **Fine-tuning:** Can be adjusted for specific tasks.
- **Generation:** Produces text based on an initial prompt.

Positive Points:

- High quality and consistency in text generation
- Versatility in various language tasks

- Ability to understand and generate content in multiple languages
- Adaptability to different writing styles and formats

Negative Points:

- May generate incorrect information or "hallucinations"
- Potential bias based on training data
- High computational cost to train and operate
- Ethical issues related to the generation of misleading content

Examples of AIs that use GPT:

- **ChatGPT:** Conversational Assistant by OpenAI
- **GPT-3 Playground:** Platform for experimenting with GPT-3
- **GitHub Copilot:** GPT-based programming assistant

DALL-E

DALL-E is an AI model that generates images from textual descriptions. It combines the power of GPT with image generation techniques. It works in a few steps:

- **Text and image encoding:** Transforms text and images into a common representation
- **Generation:** Creates images pixel by pixel based on the textual description

- **Refinement:** Applies techniques to improve image quality and coherence

Positive Points:

- Ability to generate highly creative and unique images
- Accurate interpretation of complex textual descriptions
- Versatility in artistic styles and concepts
- Potential to accelerate design and illustration processes

Negative Points:

- May produce images with artifacts or inconsistencies
- Limitations in generating very specific details
- Copyright and Intellectual Property Issues
- Potential misuse to create misleading or offensive images

Examples of AIs that use DALL-E:

- **DALL-E 2:** Advanced version of OpenAI's original DALL-E
- **Midjourney:** While it doesn't exactly use DALL-E, it uses similar principles
- **Craiyon (formerly DALL-E mini):** More affordable and open source version

Stable Diffusion

Stable Diffusion is an imaging model that uses a diffusion process to create images from noise. It works in a few steps:

- **Diffusion Process:** Gradually adds noise to an image
- **Reverse Training:** Learn to reverse the noise process

- **Generation:** Creates images by starting with noise and gradually removing it

Positive Points:

- Generates high-quality images with less computational resources
- Open source, allowing greater accessibility and customization
- Versatility in different styles and types of images
- Ability to edit and manipulate existing images

Negative Points:

- May have difficulty with certain types of details or abstract concepts
- Ethical issues related to the generation of controversial content
- Potential for misuse in creating deepfakes
- Challenges of fine control over the outcome

Examples of AIs that use Stable Diffusion:

- Stable Diffusion Web UI: Popular interface to use the model
- DreamStudio: Stability AI's platform for imaging
- Canva Text to Image: Canva integrated tool using Stable Diffusion

Impact of generative AI on creative industries

Generative AI is rapidly transforming creative industries, from graphic design and music production to writing and filmmaking. This technological advancement brings with it a range of opportunities and challenges that are reshaping the way creative content is produced, distributed and consumed.

The impact of generative AI on the creative industries is profound and multifaceted. While it offers exciting opportunities to increase productivity, stimulate creativity and democratize content creation, it also presents significant challenges related to authenticity, copyright and the future of creative work.

As these technologies continue to evolve, it will be crucial for creative industries to find a balance between harnessing the potential of AI and preserving the unique value of human creativity. This may involve developing new business models, redefining creative roles, and creating ethical and legal frameworks that address the complexities of this new era of AI-assisted creation.

The future of creative industries will likely be characterized by a symbiosis between human creativity and AI capabilities, where technology serves as a powerful tool to amplify and complement, rather than replace, human ingenuity and expression. Let's now discuss the positives and negatives of these tools.

Positive Points

Increased Productivity

Generative AI can significantly speed up creative processes, allowing professionals to produce more content in less time. For example, a graphic designer can use AI tools like Midjourney to quickly generate initial concepts for a logo, saving hours of manual sketching.

Expanding Creativity

Generative AIs can serve as a source of inspiration, offering ideas and perspectives that human creators may not have initially considered, where for example a writer facing writer's block for whatever reason could use ChatGPT to generate ideas for plot, characters or settings, stimulating new directions for their story.

Democratization of Creation

AI tools make creating high-quality content more accessible to hobbyists and small businesses that may not have the resources to hire specialized professionals. For example, a small business can use Canva with its built-in AI tools to create professional marketing materials without the need for a dedicated designer.

Personalization at Scale

AI enables the creation of personalized content at scale, catering to individual preferences efficiently where music streaming platforms like Spotify use AI to generate personalized playlists for millions of users, each tailored to individual musical tastes.

Exploration of New Creative Formats

AI is enabling previously unimaginable forms of art and entertainment where artists are using generative AI to create interactive artworks that respond in real-time to the viewer's actions, creating unique and immersive experiences.

Negative Points

Devaluation of Human Creative Work

The ease and speed with which AI can generate content could lead to the devaluation of human creative work, potentially impacting jobs and pay where some companies have chosen to use AI-generated images instead of hiring photographers or illustrators for projects, reducing job opportunities for these professionals.

Copyright and Intellectual Property Issues

AI content generation raises complex questions about authorship and copyright, which have already generated several lawsuits, especially when the AI is trained on existing works and even access to paid content where visual artists have protested against the unauthorized use of their works to train AI models such as Stable Diffusion, alleging copyright infringement, or American newspapers citing that some AIs with ChatGpt consult paid content generating responses and therefore affecting financially and also the copyright of their articles.

Content Homogenization

Over-reliance on AI could lead to a certain uniformity in the content produced, potentially reducing diversity and originality in creative industries, for example in journalism the widespread use of AI tools for article generation could result in less diverse and more standardized news coverage.

Loss of Authenticity and Emotional Connection

AI-generated content can lack the emotional depth and authenticity that is often valued in human creative works, whereas a book generated entirely by AI may be technically well-written, but may fail to capture the emotional nuances and lived experiences that readers seek in quality literature.

Dilution of Expertise and Specialized Skills

The ease of using AI tools may lead to a decrease in the development of specialized creative skills, which in this author's view is the second most concerning for all humanity. For example, design students, programming students may become overly dependent on AI tools for concept generation, potentially hindering the development of their abilities to create and research new solutions.

Ethical and Representation Issues

Generative AIs can perpetuate or amplify biases present in their training data, leading to representation problems and stereotypes in creative content, for example. AI models for generating images can present gender or racial biases, producing disproportionate or stereotypical representations of certain groups in illustrations or designs. Note that to generate images it will do so based on an analysis of the data that was used for its training. If this content is polluted with some bias, some type of representation that is not seen favorably, these creations may suffer from the same problem, which in this author's view is by far the most worrying of all the problems that an AI can cause.

Let's take a hypothetical and even absurd example where, for example, I train the data mass for a GPT where examples of pets are very focused on exotic animals or even absurd "memes", for example, several texts where I have a "pet dragon" because of an existing animation.

There is a good chance that any question I ask about pets will be answered by the person that the "dragon" is one of the most common pets people have in their homes, which would clearly be absurd. This example would be wrong, but it would still be quickly identified as an error and could even be funny, but think about how many subjects can cause serious problems for users where the answer could be loaded with prejudice, political bias, criminal and/or reprehensible actions.

Artificial General Intelligence (AGI): Concept, Advances and Challenges

What is Artificial General Intelligence?

Artificial General Intelligence (AGI) refers to a type of AI that has human-like cognitive capabilities, capable of learning, adapting, and solving problems across a wide range of tasks without the need for specific reprogramming. Unlike narrow AI, which specializes in specific functions, AGI seeks to replicate the versatility of human thought, being able to understand abstract concepts, make complex decisions, and even demonstrate creativity.

The quest to develop AI is one of the main challenges in computer science and neuroscience, as it requires not only advances in machine learning and natural language processing, but also a deep understanding of how the human brain actually works.

At what level are we in the quest for AGI?

Currently, the AI we use is classified as narrow or weak AI because it is highly specialized for specific tasks, such as image recognition, natural language processing, and strategic games. Advanced algorithms such as deep neural networks and reinforcement learning models have enabled impressive achievements, but we are still far from achieving full AI.

Companies and researchers around the world, including labs like OpenAI, DeepMind, and renowned universities, are developing systems that seek to approximate AI. Advanced models like GPT-4 and its subsequent versions demonstrate significant advances in the ability to generate text, answer questions, and simulate complex conversations. However, these systems still lack true understanding of the world, consciousness, and genuine autonomy.

Artificial General Intelligence represents both a revolutionary promise and a significant challenge for the future of humanity. While we are far from achieving its full realization, continued advances in the field indicate that its development may only be a matter of time. For AI to be a benefit rather than a threat, it is essential that its creation be accompanied by robust regulations, ethical debates, and a global commitment to ensuring that this technology is used for the good of society.

Positive points of IAG

The development of a full AGI could bring significant benefits to humanity. Some of the key positive aspects include:

- **Advances in Medicine** : An AI could analyze clinical data in an extremely accurate way, helping in the discovery of new treatments, early diagnosis and personalization of therapies.

- **Intelligent Automation** : Industrial, agricultural and service sectors could be transformed with intelligent systems capable of performing complex tasks, increasing productivity and reducing costs.

- **Global Problem Solving** : Issues such as climate change, resource distribution and crisis management could be analyzed and solved more efficiently with the help of a highly developed AGI.

- **Personalized Education** : AI-based learning systems could adapt to the individual needs of each student, offering more effective and inclusive learning methods.

IAG's fears and challenges

Despite the positive potential, the development of an AGI also raises significant concerns and challenges:

- **Loss of Control** : If an AGI becomes autonomous and makes decisions without adequate human oversight, there are unpredictable risks that could compromise global security.

- **Impact on the Job Market** : With advanced intelligence capable of replacing a large part of the workforce, millions of jobs could be eliminated, generating economic and social crises.

- **Ethics and Responsibility** : How can we ensure that an AI follows moral guidelines and makes decisions that benefit humanity? Questions of algorithmic bias and control are key.

- **Cyber Security** : If misused, an AGI could be used for cyber attacks, espionage, and other threats to global security.

AI and Internet of Things (IoT)

How AI and IoT complement each other

Artificial Intelligence (AI) and the Internet of Things (IoT) are two of the most transformative technologies of our time. When combined, they create a powerful ecosystem that significantly improves people's lives in everything from healthcare to home automation. Let's explore how these technologies complement each other and the positive impact they have on everyday life.

The impact of AI and IoT will only grow as both technologies evolve. As devices and systems become ever more integrated and intelligent, we can expect to see a continued transformation in the way we live and work, fostering a more efficient, secure, and personalized society. However, it is also important to keep privacy and data security issues in mind to ensure that these advances benefit everyone.

Applications in smart homes, smart cities and industry 4.0

Developments in Artificial Intelligence (AI) and the Internet of Things (IoT) are revolutionizing how we live and work. When these technologies come together, they create smarter, more efficient, and more responsive environments. Let's explore how these innovations manifest themselves in smart homes, smart cities, and Industry 4.0.

Smart Homes

Smart homes are homes equipped with interconnected devices that automate household tasks and provide comfort, security, and energy efficiency. In smart homes, IoT devices such as security cameras, thermostats, and appliances collect data from the environment. AI processes this data to learn residents' preferences and optimize daily operations.

Examples:

- **Smart Climate Control:** Smart thermostats automatically adjust the temperature based on occupants' presence and weather conditions, learning preferences over time.
- **Home Security:** Connected cameras and sensors alert homeowners to intrusions in real time, while AI analyzes patterns to predict and prevent security incidents.
- **Virtual Assistants:** Devices like Alexa or Google Home work with other gadgets to control lights, music, and services in a fluid and integrated way.

Smart Cities

Smart cities use technology to increase the efficiency of urban services, improve sustainability and improve the quality of life of citizens. IoT sensors installed throughout the city collect data on traffic, air quality, energy consumption, among others. AI analyzes this data to optimize resources and plan effective interventions.

Examples:

- **Traffic Management:** Traffic control systems automatically adjust traffic signals to optimize flows, reduce congestion and improve safety, based on real-time data.
- **Environmental Monitoring:** Pollution sensors measure air quality and AI suggests measures to mitigate negative impacts on public health.
- **Energy Efficiency:** Smart power grids dynamically adjust energy supply to meet demand, reducing waste and costs.

Industry 4.0

Industry 4.0 represents the fourth industrial revolution, marked by automation, data exchange and agile integration between industrial systems. IoT devices in factories collect data on operations, machines and products. AI processes this information to optimize production, predict failures and improve product quality.

Examples:

- **Predictive Maintenance:** Sensors monitor the health of machines and AI predicts when maintenance will be needed, preventing unplanned downtime and saving resources.
- **Flexible Production:** Production lines automatically adjust operations according to changes in market demand, enabling a quick and effective response to new opportunities.
- **Product Quality:** AI analyzes production data to automatically identify and correct defects before they affect the product, maintaining quality standards.

The integration of AI and IoT transforms ordinary environments into self-adjusting and responsive systems, bringing significant benefits such as increased efficiency, sustainability, convenience and safety. However, implementing these technologies also requires addressing challenges such as data security and privacy, ensuring that these advances effectively serve the interests of society.

Real-time data collection and analysis

The ability to collect and analyze data in real time through the combination of IoT devices and AI algorithms is transforming the way we control and manage processes in several areas. This synergy is essential for the development of more modern and faster systems, significantly improving the quality of various aspects of human life.

The combination of IoT and AI for real-time data collection and analysis is changing established paradigms, ushering in a new era of dynamic and predictive control. This approach not only enhances existing systems but also creates opportunities for the development of futuristic solutions that will benefit humanity in a comprehensive way. However, it is imperative to address ethical and security concerns, ensuring that data privacy is respected and that the use of these advances is safe and responsible.

Data Collection via IoT

- **Interconnected Sensors and Devices:** At the heart of the IoT are millions of sensors and devices that are continuously collecting data. These devices range from simple thermometers to sophisticated drones, all connecting to the internet to transmit information.

- **Data Diversity:** IoT devices capture a wide variety of data, including temperature, air quality, motion, light, sounds, and more. This diversity allows for a comprehensive and detailed view of the monitored environments.

Real-Time Data Analysis by AI

- **Immediate Processing:** Once collected, data is transmitted to AI systems that use machine learning algorithms to process it almost instantly. This ability to analyze data in real time is crucial for responding quickly to different scenarios and events.

- **Prediction and Optimization:** AI can predict future events based on patterns detected in historical and current data. For example, it can anticipate spikes in demand in power systems or predict failures in industrial equipment.

Practical Applications

Health

- **Patient Monitoring:** Wearable sensors monitor patients' vital signs in real time, allowing AI to detect irregularities and alert healthcare professionals before emergencies occur.

Agriculture

- **Precision Agriculture:** Sensors in the field collect data on soil and weather conditions. AI analyzes this information to recommend optimal farming practices, improving productivity and sustainability.

Transport

- **Traffic Management:** Cameras and sensors on roads provide data on traffic flow. AI adjusts traffic signals in real time to reduce congestion and improve road safety.

Benefits of IoT and AI Integration

- **Improved Efficiency:** Faster, more accurate controls reduce waste and maximize resource utilization, resulting in financial and environmental savings.
- **Immediate Response:** The ability to process data in real time enables quick decisions, which are vital in critical situations, such as natural disasters or medical emergencies.
- **Continuous Innovation:** Constant data analysis promotes innovation, as AI can identify new trends and insights for continuous process improvements.

Tools and Technologies for AI

Artificial Intelligence development has a rich ecosystem of frameworks and libraries that facilitate the creation and implementation of complex models. Here are some of the most popular ones, along with short examples of how they are used. These frameworks and libraries form the backbone of many AI projects in various areas, such as computer vision, natural language processing, and robotics, and as you can see, the vast majority are designed to run in Python.

Each offers unique tools that meet specific developer needs, facilitating innovation and agile development of AI solutions.

Best Frameworks and Libraries for Developers

TensorFlow

Developed by Google, TensorFlow is one of the most widely used libraries for machine learning and deep learning. It is known for its flexibility and scalability.

Example of Usage in python:

```python
import tensorflow as tf

# Criação de um modelo sequencial
model = tf.keras.models.Sequential([
    tf.keras.layers.Dense(128, activation='relu', input_shape=(784,)),
    tf.keras.layers.Dense(10, activation='softmax')
])

# Compilação do modelo
model.compile(optimizer='adam',
        loss='sparse_categorical_crossentropy',
        metrics=['accuracy'])

# Treinamento do modelo
model.fit(x_train, y_train, epochs=5)
```

PyTorch

Created by Facebook AI Research (FAIR), PyTorch is known for its ease of use and dynamism. It allows for rapid experimentation and is often used for research.

Example of Usage in python:

```python
import torch
import torch.nn as nn
import torch.optim as optim

# Definição de um modelo simples
class SimpleNN(nn.Module):
    def __init__(self):
        super(SimpleNN, self).__init__
        self.fc = nn.Linear(784, 10)

    def forward(self, x):
        return self.fc(x)

model = SimpleNN

# Definição de loss e optimizer
criterion = nn.CrossEntropyLoss
optimizer = optim.Adam(model.parameters)

# Treinamento do modelo
for epoch in range(num_epochs):
    optimizer.zero_grad
    outputs = model(x_train)
    loss = criterion(outputs, y_train)
    loss.backward
    optimizer.step
```

Keras

Keras is a high-level API for neural networks, easy to use and integrate into frameworks like TensorFlow.

Example of Usage in python:

```python
from keras.models import Sequential
from keras.layers import Dense

# Criação de um modelo sequencial
model = Sequential
model.add(Dense(128, activation='relu', input_dim=784))
model.add(Dense(10, activation='softmax'))

# Compilação do modelo
model.compile(optimizer='adam',
        loss='sparse_categorical_crossentropy',
        metrics=['accuracy'])

# Treinamento do modelo
model.fit(x_train, y_train, epochs=5)
```

Scikit-learn

Scikit-learn is a machine learning library in Python, especially suited for statistical models and supervised learning.

```python
from sklearn.datasets import load_iris
from sklearn.model_selection import train_test_split
from sklearn.ensemble import RandomForestClassifier
from sklearn.metrics import accuracy_score

# Carregar dados
iris = load_iris
X_train, X_test, y_train, y_test = train_test_split(iris.data, iris.target, test_size=0.3)

# Criar um classificador RandomForest
clf = RandomForestClassifier

# Treinar o modelo
clf.fit(X_train, y_train)

# Prever e avaliar
y_pred = clf.predict(X_test)
print("Accuracy:", accuracy_score(y_test, y_pred))
```

OpenCV

OpenCV is a library for image processing and computer vision. Widely used in AI applications involving computer vision.

Example of Usage in python:

```python
import cv2

# Carregar uma imagem
image = cv2.imread('image.jpg')

# Converter para escala de cinza
gray_image = cv2.cvtColor(image, cv2.COLOR_BGR2GRAY)

# Exibir a imagem
cv2.imshow('Gray Image', gray_image)
cv2.waitKey(0)
cv2.destroyAllWindows
```

Cloud AI Platforms: AWS, Google Cloud, Azure

In today's world, Artificial Intelligence (AI) is becoming increasingly present in our lives, often in ways we don't even realize. The major cloud computing platforms—Amazon Web Services (AWS), Google Cloud, and Microsoft Azure—offer a wide range of AI services that power many of the technologies we use every day. Let's explore each of these platforms, their most notable AI services, and how they impact our daily lives.

Amazon Web Services (AWS)

AWS is a leader in cloud services and offers a variety of AI and machine learning tools.

Featured Services:

- **Amazon Rekognition:** Image and video analysis for facial recognition, object detection, and scene analysis.
- **Amazon Lex:** Building chatbots and conversational interfaces.
- **Amazon Polly:** Text-to-speech with natural voices.
- **Amazon SageMaker:** Platform for building, training, and deploying machine learning models.

Everyday Applications:

- Facial recognition security systems in airports and buildings.
- Virtual assistants on e-commerce sites.
- Audiobook narration and accessible content.
- Personalized recommendations on streaming platforms.

Google Cloud

Google Cloud Platform (GCP) offers a range of AI services based on technology that Google uses in its own products.

Featured Services:

- **Vision AI:** Image analysis for object, face and text detection.
- **Speech-to-Text and Text-to-Speech:** Bidirectional conversion between speech and text.
- **Natural Language AI:** Sentiment analysis and entity extraction in text.
- **AutoML:** Creating custom machine learning models without requiring AI expertise.

Everyday Applications:

- Automatic translation in messaging applications and social networks.
- Automatic video transcription and captions on YouTube.
- Google voice assistant on smartphones and smart home devices.
- Improved photo quality on Android smartphones.

Microsoft Azure

Microsoft's Azure platform offers a wide range of AI services, many of which are integrated into existing Microsoft products.

Featured Services:

- **Azure Cognitive Services:** Set of APIs [6]for vision, speech, language, and decision making.
- **Azure Bot Service:** Developing [7]intelligent chatbots.
- **Azure Machine Learning:** Platform for creating and managing machine learning models.
- **Azure Cognitive Search:** Search service with AI capabilities for content analysis.

Everyday Applications:

- Cortana virtual assistant on Windows devices.
- Translation and dictionary features in Microsoft Office.

---

[6]*APIs (Application Programming Interfaces) are sets of rules and protocols that enable communication between different systems or software. They allow applications to access features or data from other services in a standardized way.*
[7]*Chatbots are artificial intelligence systems designed to simulate conversations with users, automatically answering questions and interacting naturally. They are used across a variety of platforms for customer service, support and task automation.*

- Spam filters and phishing detection [8]in Outlook.
- Personalized recommendations on the LinkedIn social network.

Impact on Daily Life

These cloud-based AI platforms are behind many technologies we use every day, often without even realizing it. Some examples include:

- **Social Networks:** Content recommendation algorithms, photo filters and facial recognition.
- **E-commerce:** Product recommendation systems, chatbots for customer service and comment analysis.
- **Media Streaming:** Personalized movie, series and music recommendations.
- **Smart Devices:** Voice assistants such as Alexa (AWS), Google Assistant (Google Cloud) and Cortana (Azure).
- **Mobility Applications:** Route optimization and demand forecasting in transportation apps.
- **Health:** Analysis of medical images for early detection of diseases.
- **Finance:** Fraud detection in banking transactions and credit risk analysis.

Cloud AI platforms from AWS, Google Cloud, and Azure are at the forefront of the AI revolution, providing the tools and infrastructure needed for businesses of all sizes to implement AI solutions. These

---

[8] *Phishing is a fraudulent cybercrime technique where attackers attempt to trick victims into providing sensitive information, such as passwords and banking details, usually through spoofed emails or websites.*

technologies are rapidly transforming the way we interact with devices, consume content, and perform everyday tasks.

As these platforms continue to evolve and become more accessible, we can expect to see even more innovations and applications of AI in our daily lives. It is therefore important to be aware of these technologies and how they are shaping our world, both to harness their benefits and to understand their ethical and social implications.

Tools for data analysis and visualization

Tableau

One of the most popular data visualization tools, with integrated AI capabilities including "Explain Data" for automatic outlier analysis and "Ask Data" for natural language queries. It is useful for creating interactive dashboards and complex visual analyses.

Power BI

Microsoft tool for business analysis and data visualization that includes "Quick Insights" for automatic pattern detection and "Q&A" for natural language queries.

Widely used Integration with Microsoft ecosystem and business analysis with integration with several other software / ERP's.[9]

---

[9] *ERP (Enterprise Resource Planning) is an integrated business management system that brings together and organizes information and processes from different areas of the company, such as finance, human resources, inventory and sales, on a single platform. The goal is to improve efficiency and decision-making.*

IBM Watson Studio

Comprehensive platform for data science and machine learning that offers automated modeling, AI-assisted data preparation, and intelligent visualizations, and is widely used in large-scale data science projects and predictive analytics.

Google Data Studio

Free Google tool for creating reports and dashboards that has AI features for integration with Google Analytics for automatic insights and predictions. Widely used for digital marketing data analysis and integration with Google products.

RapidMiner

Data science platform that combines data preparation, machine learning, and model deployment with AI capabilities: ML workflow automation, automatic model selection. Used by users looking for a complete data science solution with little coding.

Plotly

Interactive data visualization library with support for multiple programming languages that contains easy integration with ML libraries like scikit-learn for model-based visualizations and is used for developers who want to create custom interactive visualizations.

H2O.ai

Open-source AI platform focused on automated machine learning (AutoML), automatic anomaly detection, time series forecasting. Used in projects that require automated modeling and model interpretability.

How to choose the right tool for your project

Clearly Define Project Objectives:

- What are the specific questions you are trying to answer?
- What kind of insights do you hope to gain?

Assess Data Complexity:

- How much data do you need to analyze?
- How diverse are the data sources?
- Do you need to deal with real-time data?

Consider the Team's Technical Skills:

- Does your team have programming experience or do they prefer drag-and-drop interfaces?
- Is there familiarity with any specific platform?

Analyze the Integration Requirements:

- What existing systems does the tool need to integrate with?
- Is there a need for compatibility with any [10]specific technology stack?

Assess Visualization Needs:

- What types of visualizations are crucial for your project?
- Do you need interactive dashboards or static reports?

---

[10]Stack, in computing, is a data structure that stores elements sequentially, following the LIFO (Last In, First Out) rule, where the last item inserted is the first to be removed. It can also refer to the set of technologies used in a project, as in "tech stack".

Consider Budget and Scalability:

- What is the budget available for data analysis tools?
- How does the tool behave as the volume of data increases?

Check the Required AI Resources:

- Do you need specific capabilities like natural language processing, computer vision, or automated predictions?

Test the Options:

- Take advantage of free trials to try out the most promising tools.
- Create a pilot project to evaluate performance in a real-world scenario.

Consider Community and Support:

- Is there an active user community for support and resources?
- What is the quality of the documentation and official support?

Evaluate the Learning Curve:

- How long will it take for your team to become proficient with the tool?
- Are there training resources available?

Think about Security and Compliance:

- Does the tool meet your industry's security and compliance requirements?
- How is sensitive data handled?

Consider Flexibility and Customization:

- Does the tool allow customization to meet your project's specific needs?
- Is it possible to extend the functionalities through APIs or plugins?

By applying these techniques, you will be able to systematically evaluate the available options and choose the tool that best aligns with the specific needs of your AI data analysis and visualization project.

Remember that choosing the right tool can have a significant impact on the success of your project, influencing the efficiency of the analysis, the quality of the insights obtained, and the ability to effectively communicate the results. Therefore, dedicate sufficient time to this selection process and do not hesitate to carry out practical tests before making a final decision.

And also thinking about the financial issue, it is known that these tools can also be expensive, so a good analysis of pros and cons within your needs can be the difference between the viability or not of a project using AI.

Practical Applications of AI

AI in healthcare: diagnostics, surgical robotics and medical research

Artificial intelligence (AI) has had a revolutionary impact on healthcare, providing significant advances in diagnostics, surgical robotics, and medical research. In the context of diagnostics, AI has excelled in its ability to analyze large volumes of data accurately and quickly. Machine learning algorithms are used to interpret medical images, such as MRIs and CT scans, helping to identify abnormalities with an accuracy many times greater than human evaluation. This not only speeds up the diagnostic process but also increases the early detection rate of several diseases, such as cancer.

In surgical robotics, AI is improving surgical techniques and procedures, providing greater precision and control during operations. AI-powered surgical robots are capable of performing extremely precise movements, minimizing the risk of human error and allowing surgeons to perform complex surgeries with less invasiveness. This results in faster recovery times for patients and reduced post-operative complications.

In medical research, AI facilitates the development of new drugs and treatments by analyzing vast amounts of biomedical data. It enables the simulation of diverse clinical scenarios and the identification of potential therapies in a much shorter time than traditional methods. This is particularly important in public health situations that require rapid responses, such as pandemics, where the speed in identifying and developing interventions can save many lives.

Implementing AI in healthcare, however, is not without its challenges. Issues such as data security, ethics in the use of AI, and the need for appropriate regulation are important topics that need to be constantly evaluated. Despite these challenges, the potential of AI to improve diagnosis, the effectiveness of surgeries, and the conduct of research is undeniable, promising to profoundly transform healthcare as we know it today.

AI in the financial sector: risk analysis, fraud detection and trading[11]

Artificial intelligence (AI) is reshaping the financial industry, with significant impacts on risk analysis, fraud detection and trading. In the area of risk analysis, AI is being used to assess creditworthiness and predict the likelihood of default with greater accuracy than traditional methods. Advanced algorithms process large volumes of financial and consumer behavior data, enabling financial institutions to more effectively identify which customers pose a potential risk. This not only improves risk management but also enables the personalization of financial offers according to each customer's profile.

When it comes to fraud detection, AI has been a crucial tool. AI-based systems can monitor transactions in real time and identify suspicious patterns that may indicate fraudulent activity. For

---

[11]*Trading is the practice of buying and selling financial assets, such as stocks, currencies or commodities, with the aim of making a profit. It can be done by individual investors or financial institutions, using a variety of strategies and analysis tools.*

example, algorithms can detect discrepancies in transaction behavior and flag transactions that deviate from a customer's usual pattern, such as a sudden and unexpected high-value purchase in an unusual location. This real-time analysis capability helps institutions react effectively and immediately, mitigating financial losses and protecting customer assets.

In the trading domain, AI is providing a significant competitive advantage. Algorithms are used to execute high-frequency trades based on predefined criteria, quickly analyzing market data and making investment decisions in fractions of a second. Furthermore, the use of machine learning enables the development of models that can predict market movements, helping traders make more informed decisions. This data-driven approach [12]enables portfolio optimization and maximization of returns.

While the benefits of AI in the financial sector are vast, it is important to highlight the associated challenges, such as the need for transparency in algorithms and ensuring data security. Furthermore, effective regulation is essential to balance innovation with consumer protection. However, the positive impact of AI on risk analysis, fraud detection and trading is transforming the efficiency and security of the financial sector, and promises to continue to revolutionize the industry in the years to come.

AI in retail: personalizing experiences and logistics

Artificial intelligence (AI) is significantly transforming the retail industry, particularly in the areas of personalization of experiences

---

[12]*Data-driven is an approach that makes decisions based on data and analysis rather than assumptions or intuition. Data-driven companies and systems use collected information to guide their strategies and optimize processes.*

and logistics. When it comes to personalization of experiences, AI enables retailers to offer customized solutions for each customer. Using data on individual purchasing behavior and preferences, AI algorithms can create product recommendations, targeted marketing campaigns, and even exclusive offers. This not only improves the customer experience by providing more personalized and efficient service, but also increases conversion rates and builds customer loyalty by creating a stronger connection with the brand.

In the logistics field, AI is optimizing the supply chain in ways that were previously unimaginable. AI-based systems can predict demand with high accuracy, allowing retailers to adjust their inventories according to seasonal trends or sudden changes in the market. In addition, AI is being used to optimize product distribution, identifying the most efficient delivery routes, saving time and reducing costs. This translates into a more agile and less expensive logistics operation, which benefits both companies and consumers, who receive their products faster.

Furthermore, AI-powered automation of logistics processes, such as the use of robots in warehouses, is significantly reducing human error and increasing operational efficiency. AI-powered robots are able to perform repetitive tasks, such as picking and packing products, with greater accuracy and less turnaround time.

Despite these advantages, implementing AI in retail does come with its own challenges; data integrity and consumer privacy are important concerns that must be carefully managed. Ethical issues and regulatory aspects of collecting and using customer data also require constant attention from retailers.

However, the potential for AI to transform retail is immense. By creating highly personalized shopping experiences and improving logistics, AI is enabling companies to improve both operational efficiency and customer satisfaction, positioning themselves strategically in an increasingly competitive market.

AI in transportation: autonomous vehicles and route optimization

Artificial intelligence (AI) is revolutionizing the transportation industry, with major impacts on autonomous vehicles and route optimization. The concept of autonomous vehicles, or driverless cars, is one of the most exciting innovations enabled by AI. Using a combination of advanced sensors, cameras, radars, and machine learning algorithms, these vehicles are able to perceive their surroundings in real time, make decisions, and navigate safely on roads and highways. This not only has the potential to reduce the number of accidents caused by human error, but also provide greater mobility for people who have mobility difficulties or are unable to drive.

The deployment of autonomous vehicles is transforming the way we think about urban transportation, promising to reduce congestion and the need for large parking areas. In addition, the ability of autonomous vehicles to communicate with each other in an interconnected network could lead to more efficient traffic management, improving vehicle flow and saving time and fuel.

In route optimization, AI plays a crucial role by analyzing large amounts of real-time data, such as traffic conditions, weather patterns, and road updates. AI algorithms can determine the most efficient routes for deliveries and passenger transportation, significantly reducing travel time and costs. For logistics and transportation companies, this translates into more cost-effective and sustainable operations, while passengers enjoy faster and more reliable journeys.

Furthermore, route optimization is a vital component in minimizing the carbon footprint of vehicles, a growing concern in an era of increased environmental awareness. With the help of AI, it is possible to not only choose the shortest route, but also the one that consumes the least energy, contributing to greener transportation practices.

However, despite the significant potential of AI in transportation, challenges remain, especially with regard to regulation, safety and public acceptance of autonomous vehicles. Regulatory uncertainty and ethical questions about machine decision-making require continued and informed debate.

In short, AI in transportation is on track to completely transform the way we move and manage logistics, promising a safer, more efficient and sustainable future for everyone.

AI in agriculture: crop monitoring and automation

Artificial intelligence (AI) is revolutionizing the agricultural sector by improving crop monitoring and automating agricultural processes. The use of AI in crop monitoring is giving farmers unprecedented insight into their crops. Using advanced sensors, drones, and satellite imagery, detailed data on plant health, soil moisture, and pest presence can be collected. This data is then analyzed by AI algorithms that can identify potential problems before they become critical, allowing for targeted and timely interventions. This allows farmers to optimize water and fertilizer use, reducing costs and minimizing environmental impact.

In agricultural automation, AI is transforming traditionally manual tasks into automated processes, improving efficiency and reducing human labor. Agricultural machines equipped with AI technology can perform activities such as planting, harvesting and weeding with millimeter precision. The use of autonomous tractors and smart harvesters is starting to become a reality, capable of operating independently in fields, day and night, thus increasing productivity and operational efficiency.

These technologies not only increase productivity but also help address environmental and sustainability challenges. By reducing the use of chemical inputs and optimizing natural resources, AI-powered precision agriculture contributes to more sustainable and environmentally friendly farming practices. Additionally, using AI to predict climate change and weather patterns also allows farmers to better prepare for adversities by protecting their crops from extreme weather events.

However, the successful integration of AI into agriculture depends on the right technological infrastructure, which remains a challenge in less developed rural areas. The initial cost of implementation and the need for technical skills are also barriers that many farmers face.

However, the positive impact of AI on agriculture is clear. By enabling more accurate monitoring and efficient automation, AI is shaping the future of agriculture, promoting smarter and more sustainable production, and ensuring food security in a world with an ever-growing population.

Ethics and Challenges of AI

The rapid expansion of artificial intelligence (AI) into various sectors of society brings with it a number of challenges and ethical considerations that need to be addressed to ensure its responsible and beneficial use. One of the main challenges is the issue of transparency. Many AI algorithms, especially those based on machine learning, operate as "black boxes" where the decision-making process is poorly understood, even by their creators. This raises concerns about liability, as it becomes difficult to determine who is to blame if the AI makes a harmful decision.

Furthermore, widespread adoption of AI could exacerbate social inequality. Entire sectors of the workforce could be automated, resulting in significant unemployment for workers in traditional occupations. To mitigate this impact, it is essential that governments and industries work together to develop reskilling and new job creation strategies that leverage human skills in ways that complement technology.

Ethics in the use of AI also encompasses privacy. AI systems often rely on large volumes of data, much of which is personal and sensitive. Improper handling and storage of this data can lead to serious privacy violations, requiring the implementation of strict regulations on data protection and informed consent.

Finally, autonomous decision-making by AI systems presents ethical dilemmas, especially in critical fields like medicine where human life may be at stake. Questions about machine autonomy versus human intervention need to be clearly defined to ensure that AI is acting in the best interests of humanity.

As a society, addressing these ethical challenges and dilemmas requires a collaborative approach involving technology developers, policymakers, ethicists [13], and the public. Only through careful and responsible governance can we ensure that AI is used equitably, safely, and ethically, reaping its benefits while minimizing its risks.

Bias in algorithms and its consequences

With the rapid adoption of artificial intelligence (AI) in a variety of areas, from recommendation systems on streaming platforms to credit decision-making and healthcare applications, the issue of algorithmic bias has gained prominence as one of the greatest ethical and technical challenges of our time. Bias in algorithms occurs when AI systems reproduce or amplify biases present in the data they were trained on. This phenomenon, if not adequately addressed, can lead to significant inequalities and large-scale discrimination.

Bias in AI algorithms is not just a technical problem, but a social and ethical challenge that has profound implications for society as a whole. While the path to solving these problems is complex and multifaceted, it is crucial that we move forward with initiatives that ensure that AI benefits everyone equitably. With a proactive and collaborative approach, we can not only mitigate the effects of algorithmic bias, but also use AI as a powerful tool for advancing social justice and equity.

---

[13]*Ethicists are professionals or scholars who dedicate themselves to the study and application of ethics, addressing moral issues, responsibilities and values in human actions, including areas such as philosophy, science and business.*

Consequences of Algorithmic Bias

Inequality in the Labor Market

The use of algorithms to screen resumes and evaluate candidates is becoming more common. However, if the historical data used to train these systems contains biases—for example, underrepresentation of minority groups in specific roles—the algorithms can perpetuate these inequities. This results in the exclusion of qualified candidates from already marginalized social groups.

Discrimination in Financial Products and Services

Credit algorithms that use historical data to determine loan eligibility or set credit limits can discriminate against certain demographic groups. If specific communities have historically faced financial hardship, algorithms may mistakenly associate them with higher credit risk. This can lead to a perpetuation of financial disparities, further exacerbating economic inequalities.

Damage to Public Safety

In some jurisdictions, algorithms are used to predict criminal activity or determine sentencing decisions. When trained on historical arrest data, which may reflect excessive patrolling of certain communities, these algorithms end up reinforcing and legitimizing discriminatory practices. This can result in disproportionate surveillance of certain areas, exacerbating social tensions and distrust between communities and law enforcement.

Impact on Health

AI systems used in medical diagnosis and treatment recommendations may also reflect bias if they are trained on data that is not representative of all populations. This can result in inaccurate diagnoses for racial minorities or ethnic groups that are underrepresented in healthcare datasets, leading to inappropriate treatments and disparities in health outcomes.

Ways to Solve the Problem

Diversity in Training Data

One of the most straightforward solutions to combating algorithmic bias is to ensure that the data used to train AI models is representative and diverse. This involves systematically collecting data that includes a wide range of demographic, behavioral, and contextual variables. Additionally, it is crucial to regularly audit datasets to identify and minimize existing biases.

Transparency and Explainability in Algorithms

Organizations using IAM should adopt transparency practices to enable users and stakeholders to understand how decisions are made. Explainability in algorithms—that is, the ability of AI systems to explain their decisions in understandable terms—becomes crucial to identifying and correcting bias.

Implementation of Regulations and Ethical Standards

Governments and regulators should develop and enforce guidelines that require companies to address bias in their algorithms. Ethical standards for the development and use of AI can help prevent and mitigate the negative impacts of bias, ensuring that AI is used fairly and responsibly.

Multidisciplinary and Collaborative Involvement

Addressing algorithmic bias requires a collaborative approach that includes technology experts, ethicists, policymakers, and representatives of affected communities. Integrating diverse perspectives into AI development can help predict and prevent unintended consequences, fostering the creation of more inclusive solutions.

Education and Awareness

Educating AI developers, companies, and the public about the complexities and implications of algorithmic bias is essential. By raising awareness of these challenges, we can foster a more conscious and ethical AI development culture.

Data Privacy and Security

In the digital age, artificial intelligence (AI) has become an integral part of our daily lives, offering innovative solutions in a variety of areas, such as healthcare, finance, transportation, and entertainment. However, as AI advances, significant concerns about data privacy and security have emerged. The extensive collection of personal data, which is essential for the functioning of most AI systems, poses potential risks of privacy and data security breaches. The balance between technological innovation and the protection of fundamental rights of individuals, such as privacy, therefore becomes a critical priority.

Data Privacy Challenges

Data privacy refers to how personal data is collected, processed and protected. With AI algorithms learning from vast amounts of data, including sensitive personal information, concerns about the control and misuse of this data are growing. Issues of consent are also central, as users may often not be fully aware of how their data is being used or may be used in the future.

Furthermore, AI systems often require large amounts of data to improve their accuracy and efficiency, potentially encouraging inappropriate data collection practices or sharing between different entities without the proper consent of data subjects.

Security Challenges

Security in the use of AI is paramount to ensure that systems are not exploited by malicious actors. Cyberattacks can corrupt AI models or use them to distribute false or compromising information. Furthermore, if not properly secured, systems that rely on AI can be manipulated to access sensitive data, compromising personal or corporate security.

Real Cases of Privacy and Security Issues

Cambridge Analytica case

One of the most notorious examples of data privacy violations involves Cambridge Analytica, which improperly collected data from millions of Facebook users without their explicit consent. This data was used to influence decisions in election campaigns, raising concerns about voter choice and manipulation through personalized campaigns. The case has sparked a global debate about privacy rights and the ethics of data collection on social media platforms.

Attack on Facial Recognition System

Another example is the attack on facial recognition systems used by governments and companies. In 2019, hackers managed to access a facial recognition database from a third-party company working for U.S. Customs, compromising photos of travelers and some personal information. Such events highlight the vulnerability of systems that handle sensitive biometric data, reinforcing the need for robust security measures.

Health Data Leakage

In the healthcare sector, there was a significant case in 2020 where the personal information of millions of patients from a major healthcare provider was exposed due to inadequate security settings in an AI platform used to assess diagnoses. This failure potentially compromised patient privacy and highlighted the urgent need for stricter security protocols in medical data environments.

Impact of AI on the job market

Artificial Intelligence (AI) is transforming the job market in profound and multifaceted ways. From automating repetitive tasks to creating new professions, AI is redefining how, where, and by whom work is done. This article explores the main impacts of AI on the job market, divided into benefits, challenges, and future prospects.

Automation of Repetitive Tasks

AI is extremely efficient at automating repetitive and routine tasks, which leads to productivity gains and cost reductions for companies. Industries such as manufacturing, logistics and customer service are already reaping the benefits of this transformation.

Example: AI-powered robots are being used on assembly lines to perform tasks like welding and painting with greater precision and speed.

Impact: Reduction in the need for labor for manual and repetitive tasks.

Creation of New Professions

While some roles are being automated, AI is also opening doors to new professions. AI specialists, data scientists, machine learning engineers, and technology ethicists are in high demand.

Example: The need for professionals who can train, manage and interpret AI systems is growing exponentially.

Impact: Emergence of career opportunities in areas that did not previously exist.

Increased Efficiency and Innovation

AI enables companies to analyze large volumes of data in real time, which facilitates strategic decision-making and the development of innovative products.

Example: Healthcare companies are using AI to analyze patient data and predict diseases before they manifest.

Impact: Improved operational efficiency and advances in sectors such as medicine, finance and education.

Challenges for Workers

Despite the benefits, AI also presents significant challenges, especially for workers whose skills may become obsolete.

Example: Employees in administrative or customer service positions can be replaced by automated systems.

Impact: Need for retraining so that workers can adapt to new market demands.

Changes in Work Dynamics

AI is driving a change in work dynamics, with greater flexibility and the possibility of remote work. AI platforms facilitate global collaboration and distributed team management.

Example: Machine translation tools and AI-powered virtual meetings are eliminating geographic barriers.

Impact: Greater inclusion and diversity in the job market.

Inequality and Social Impacts

AI can widen social inequalities, as it mainly benefits developed countries and companies with access to advanced technology. In addition, the concentration of wealth in the hands of technology companies is a growing concern.

Example: Large technology corporations are accumulating economic power and political influence.

Impact: Need for public policies to ensure a fair distribution of the benefits of AI.

Future Perspectives

The future of AI work will be marked by greater collaboration between humans and machines. AI will not completely replace humans, but it will act as a tool to augment our capabilities.

Example: Healthcare professionals will use AI to diagnose diseases, but human contact will remain essential in patient care.

Impact: A balanced approach that combines technology and human skills will be crucial.

Responsibility and regulation

As Artificial Intelligence (AI) becomes increasingly present in the workplace, critical questions about ethical, legal, and social responsibilities arise. The absence of adequate regulation can lead to abuse, discrimination, and inequalities. This supplement addresses key responsibilities and the need for regulation to ensure that AI is used in a fair and beneficial manner.

Corporate Responsibilities

Companies adopting AI solutions have a responsibility to ensure that these technologies are used ethically and transparently.

- **Transparency:** Companies should be clear about how AI is used in hiring, performance evaluation, and decision-making processes. Example: Candidate selection algorithms should be audited to avoid racial or gender bias.
- **Data Protection:** AI often relies on large volumes of data, which requires companies to ensure the privacy and security of this information. For example, companies must comply with regulations such as the GDPR (General Data Protection Regulation) in Europe.

Government Responsibilities

Governments have a crucial role in creating policies and regulations that promote the ethical use of AI.

- **Anti-Discrimination Legislation:** Laws must be created or updated to ensure that AI systems do not perpetuate or amplify inequalities. Example: Prohibit the use of algorithms that discriminate based on race, gender, or age.
- **Incentives for Reskilling:** Governments should provide training and education programs to help workers adapt to the changes brought about by AI. Example: Partnering with educational institutions to offer courses in data science and programming.

Responsibilities of AI Developers

Creators and developers of AI systems have an obligation to ensure that their technologies are fair, safe, and transparent.

- **Testing and Auditing:** AI systems must be rigorously tested to identify and correct biases. Example: Using [14]diverse datasets to train facial recognition algorithms.
- **Accountability:** Developers should be held accountable for failures or damages caused by their systems. Example: In cases of automated decisions that result in harm, developers should be able to explain how the system reached that conclusion.

---

[14]Datasets are organized sets of data, usually structured in tables or files, that are used for analysis, training machine learning models, or experiments. They can contain information from a variety of sources and are essential for making data-driven decisions.

Need for Global Regulation

AI is a technology that transcends borders, which makes the creation of international standards and regulations essential.

- **Ethical Standards:** Organizations such as UNESCO and the OECD are working on global guidelines for the ethical use of AI. Example: The OECD Declaration of Principles on AI sets standards for transparency, fairness, and accountability.
- **Worker Protection:** Regulations must protect workers' rights in an increasingly automated market. Example: Ensure that automation does not lead to mass layoffs without adequate compensation.

Regulatory Challenges

Regulating AI is not a simple task, as it involves balancing innovation with social and ethical protection.

- **Speed of Innovation:** Technology advances quickly, while laws tend to move more slowly. Example: AI-specific laws may become obsolete before they are even implemented.
- **Technical Complexity:** Regulators often lack the technical expertise needed to fully understand AI systems. Example: Need for consultation with technology and ethics experts.

Examples of Ongoing Regulation

Some countries and organizations are already taking steps to regulate the use of AI in the labor market.

- **European Union:** The Artificial Intelligence Act proposes to categorize AI systems based on the risk they pose and impose restrictions as necessary.
- **United States:** The Algorithmic Accountability Act aims to require companies to assess the impact of their algorithms on issues such as discrimination and privacy.
- **Brazil:** The AI Legal Framework under discussion in Congress, with a focus on fundamental rights and transparency.

A balanced future depends on collaboration between all stakeholders to create an AI ecosystem that fosters innovation without compromising workers' rights and dignity.

AI Trends and Future

Quantum AI: the next technological leap

Quantum AI is an emerging field that combines artificial intelligence (AI) with quantum computing to create more powerful and efficient information processing systems. Quantum computing is based on the principles of quantum mechanics, which allow subatomic particles to exist in multiple states at the same time, enabling complex calculations to be performed faster than classical computers.

Quantum AI is an emerging field that combines artificial intelligence with quantum computing to create more powerful and efficient information processing systems. While there are still challenges and limitations to be overcome, quantum AI has the potential to revolutionize many areas, including healthcare, finance, and cybersecurity.

Real Examples of Quantum AI

- **IBM Quantum Experience:** IBM offers a cloud-based quantum computing platform that enables developers to build and run quantum algorithms. The platform includes tools for developing quantum AI, such as Qiskit, a software framework for building quantum applications.
- **Google Quantum AI Lab:** Google has created a quantum AI lab that aims to develop practical applications for quantum computing. The lab works on projects such as creating quantum algorithms for solving optimization problems and implementing quantum neural networks.
- **Microsoft Quantum:** Microsoft has developed a quantum computing platform that includes tools for developing quantum AI, such as Q# (Q Sharp), a programming language for creating quantum applications.

Quantum AI Applications

Quantum AI has the potential to revolutionize several areas, including:

- **Healthcare:** Quantum AI can be used to analyze complex medical data, such as MRI images and DNA sequences.
- **Finance:** Quantum AI can be used for complex financial data analysis, such as market predictions and risk management.

- **Cybersecurity:** Quantum AI can be used to create more secure encryption algorithms and to detect cyberattacks.

Challenges and Limitations of Quantum AI

While quantum AI has the potential to revolutionize many areas, there are still challenges and limitations to overcome, including:

- **Number of qubits** [15]**:** Currently, quantum computers have a limited number of qubits, which limits the complexity of the problems that can be solved.
- **Quantum error:** Quantum AI is sensitive to quantum errors, which can affect the accuracy of results.
- **Lack of experts:** Quantum AI is an emerging field, and there is a lack of qualified experts to develop and apply these technologies.

Explainable AI (XAI): How to improve the transparency of models

Artificial Intelligence (AI) is revolutionizing many areas, from healthcare to finance, but the lack of transparency and

---

[15]*Qubits (or quantum bits) are the fundamental units of information in quantum computing. Unlike classical bits, which can only have two values (0 or 1), qubits can exist in multiple states at the same time, known as superposition. This allows qubits to process information more efficiently and faster than classical computers.*

Example:
Think of a classical bit as a coin that can be either heads (0) or tails (1). A qubit is like a coin that can be either heads, tails, or both at the same time, allowing for more options and flexibility in complex computations.

explainability in its decision-making processes is a major obstacle to adoption and trust in its solutions. This is where Explainable Artificial Intelligence (XAI) comes in, an emerging field that aims to create AI systems that are transparent, explainable, and understandable.

What is XAI?

XAI is a set of techniques and methods that aim to explain how AI systems make decisions. This includes identifying the factors that influence decisions, analyzing the data used, and explaining the reasoning processes used. XAI aims to provide a clear and understandable view of how AI systems work, allowing users to understand and trust their decisions.

Why is it important?

XAI is critical to ensuring trust and adoption of AI systems in a variety of areas, including:

- **Healthcare:** XAI can help explain diagnoses and treatments recommended by AI systems, allowing doctors and patients to better understand decisions.
- **Finance:** XAI can help explain credit and investment decisions, enabling clients to better understand risks and opportunities.
- **Transportation:** XAI can help explain navigation and control decisions of autonomous vehicles, allowing passengers to better understand the vehicle's actions.

XAI Techniques

There are several XAI techniques, including:

- **Interpretation modeling:** technique that aims to create models that are understandable and explainable.
- **Sensitivity analysis:** technique that aims to identify the factors that influence the AI system's decisions.
- **Feature explanation:** technique that aims to explain the characteristics of data that influence the AI system's decisions.

Challenges and Limitations

Although XAI is an emerging and promising field, there are still challenges and limitations to overcome, including:

- **Complexity:** AI systems are increasingly complex, making it difficult to explain their decisions.
- **Privacy:** XAI can compromise data privacy, making it necessary to develop techniques to protect data.
- **Interpretation:** XAI can be interpreted in different ways, making it necessary to develop techniques to ensure correct interpretation.

AI and Sustainability: How AI Can Help the Environment

Artificial Intelligence (AI) has hundreds and thousands of positives as we are seeing, but its impact on the environment is an increasingly important topic. AI can be a powerful tool to help protect the environment, but it can also have negative impacts if not used responsibly, but we also need to address the problems it causes.

How can AI help the environment?

- **Natural resource monitoring:** AI can be used to monitor natural resources such as forests, oceans and the atmosphere, helping to detect changes and predict problems.
- **Energy efficiency:** AI can be used to optimize energy efficiency in buildings and industries, reducing energy consumption and greenhouse gas emissions.
- **Waste management:** AI can be used to optimize waste management, helping to reduce the amount of waste sent to landfills.
- **Biodiversity conservation:** AI can be used to monitor and protect biodiversity, helping to identify threatened species and develop conservation plans.

Where is AI harming the environment?

- **High energy consumption:** AI requires large amounts of energy to function, which can contribute to greenhouse gas emissions and climate change.
- **E-waste [16]:** AI can contribute to the generation of e-waste, or electronic waste, which can be difficult to recycle and can contaminate the environment.
- **Unsustainable development:** AI can be used to develop technologies that are not sustainable, such as

---

[16] E-waste is the disposal of obsolete or broken electronic devices, such as cell phones, computers and batteries, which may contain toxic and recyclable materials.

cryptocurrency mining, which can contribute to climate change.

Solutions for a more sustainable future

- **Sustainable AI Development:** It is important to develop AI that is sustainable and considers the environmental impact of its actions.
- **Use of renewable energy:** It is important to use renewable energy to power AI, thus reducing greenhouse gas emissions.
- **Reducing energy consumption:** It is important to reduce AI energy consumption using techniques such as energy efficiency and process optimization.
- **E-waste recycling:** It is important to develop e-waste recycling programs to reduce the amount of electronic waste that is generated.

Predictions for the coming years

Artificial intelligence (AI) has been advancing rapidly in recent years, impacting sectors such as healthcare, manufacturing, finance and entertainment. With the advancement of machine learning models, we are moving towards a future in which AI will become increasingly integrated into everyday life, playing key roles in automating processes, personalizing experiences and making strategic decisions.

One of the main advances expected is the evolution of generative AI, capable of creating complex content, such as texts, images and even programming codes with increasingly human-like quality. This could revolutionize creative sectors, enabling the automated production of advertising materials, scripts and even digital works of art. However, it also brings challenges, such as the spread of misinformation and the need for regulations to prevent the misuse of technology.

In the healthcare sector, AI promises faster and more accurate diagnoses, helping doctors identify diseases early and develop personalized treatments. Combined with robotics, it can improve surgeries and hospital care, reducing errors and increasing the efficiency of procedures. In the industrial sector, AI-based automation tends to optimize production lines, reduce costs and increase safety in the workplace.

On the other hand, there are concerns about the impact of AI on the job market. Many repetitive roles could be replaced by intelligent systems, requiring professionals to retrain for new areas. In addition, ethical issues such as data privacy and algorithmic bias will continue to be critical topics for global debate.

In the long term, researchers are seeking to develop so-called artificial general intelligence (AGI), which would have human-like cognitive capabilities and be able to learn and reason broadly. If this goal is to be achieved, clear guidelines will need to be established to ensure that AI is used safely and in a way that benefits society.

Given this scenario, it is essential that governments, companies and the academic community work together to shape a future in which AI contributes to collective well-being, promoting technological advances without compromising ethical and social values. The challenge lies in balancing innovation and responsibility, ensuring that artificial intelligence is an ally of humanity in the coming decades.

How to Become an AI Professional

Artificial intelligence (AI) is transforming many industries and creating job opportunities. To work in this field, it is essential to develop specific skills, from using AI tools to achieve results to creating and training advanced models. The skills required vary according to the level of involvement with the technology, ranging from users who apply AI in their daily lives to professionals who develop new intelligent solutions.

Skills needed to work with AI

Skills for AI Users

AI users are those who use artificial intelligence-based tools to optimize tasks and processes. Key skills for this group include:

1. **Familiarity with AI Tools** : Know how to use platforms such as ChatGPT, Midjourney and DALL·E for content generation and task automation.

2. **Results Interpretation and Curation** : Ability to assess the quality of AI-generated responses and refine them as needed.

3. **Prompt Engineering** : Know how to craft effective commands to obtain more accurate and useful responses from generative AI systems.

4. **Ethics and Critical Awareness** : Understanding the impacts of AI including algorithmic bias and privacy issues, ensuring responsible use.

Skills for Professionals Training AI Models

Professionals working on training and improving AI models require more advanced technical skills, including:

1. **Programming Languages** : Solid knowledge of Python, R and frameworks such as TensorFlow and PyTorch for developing machine learning models.

2. **Data Manipulation** : Ability to process and clean large volumes of data using libraries such as Pandas and NumPy.

3. **Statistical and Mathematical Modeling** : Understanding linear algebra, calculus, and statistics to improve the accuracy of AI models.

4. **Model Training and Tuning** : Knowledge of hyperparameters, cross-validation, and optimization techniques to create more efficient models.

5. **API and Integration Development** : Ability to deploy models into real applications using APIs and scalable architectures.

Skills for AI Creators

AI creators are professionals who design new architectures and models of artificial intelligence. Their skills require in-depth knowledge of:

1. **Deep Learning Research** : Domain of convolutional neural networks (CNNs), recurrent networks (RNNs) and transformer models such as GPT and BERT.

2. **High Performance Computing** : Using GPUs and TPUs to process large volumes of data and train advanced neural networks.

3. **Artificial General Intelligence (AGI)** : Research on the evolution of AI to achieve cognitive capabilities closer to human intelligence.

4. **AI Ethics and Governance** : Defining guidelines for safe and responsible development of technology.

5. **Creation of New Algorithms** : Development of new methods for machine learning, expanding the limits of current AI.

Recommended courses, certifications, and resources

Artificial Intelligence (AI) has revolutionized many areas and offers opportunities for professionals at different levels of experience. Whether you are a user applying AI to optimize processes, an expert in model training, or a developer looking to create your own AI solutions, there are courses and certifications that can help you achieve your goals.

No matter your experience level, there's a learning path that's right for you. Investing in AI knowledge can open doors to incredible opportunities and enhance your ability to use, train, and develop cutting-edge AI.

For Professionals who apply AI to Generate Results

If you want to use AI tools to optimize tasks, automate processes, or improve decision making, the following courses may be useful:

- **Google AI for Everyone (Coursera):** Introduction to AI and its practical applications.
- **AI Business School (Microsoft):** AI applications in the corporate world.
- **Prompt Engineering for ChatGPT (DeepLearning.AI):** Techniques to maximize the use of generative AI.
- **Data Science and AI for Business (Udemy):** Practical approach to applying AI in different industries.

Recommended Certifications:

- **AI-900: Microsoft Azure AI Fundamentals:** Certification to understand the fundamental concepts of AI.
- **Google Cloud Machine Learning Engineer:** For professionals who use AI in Google Cloud services.

For Professionals Training AI Models

If you want to dive deeper into training AI and machine learning models, consider the following courses:

- **Machine Learning (Andrew Ng - Coursera):** Classic course on machine learning.
- **Deep Learning Specialization (DeepLearning.AI):** Advanced course on neural networks and deep learning.
- **MLOps (DataCamp, Coursera):** Best practices for deploying and maintaining AI models.

- **TensorFlow Developer Certificate Training (Udemy, TensorFlow):** For those who want to work with TensorFlow and advanced deep learning models.

Recommended Certifications:

- **TensorFlow Developer Certificate:** To demonstrate skills in deep learning.
- **AWS Certified Machine Learning – Specialty:** Focused on training and deploying models on AWS.
- **Microsoft Certified: Azure AI Engineer Associate:** For professionals who train and deploy AI in the cloud.

For Professionals Who Create and Develop AI Models

If your goal is to develop new AI models or improve existing algorithms, consider the following courses:

- **CS50's Introduction to Artificial Intelligence with Python (Harvard - edX):** Introductory AI course with Python.
- **Advanced Machine Learning (Coursera - Moscow University):** Advanced techniques for AI development.
- **Reinforcement Learning Specialization (DeepLearning.AI):** Specific approach to reinforcement learning.
- **Generative AI with LLMs (Google Cloud, DeepLearning.AI):** Creating advanced generative models.

Recommended Certifications:

- **Professional Machine Learning Engineer (Google Cloud):** For experts in building robust AI models.
- **OpenAI API Certification:** For developers building applications with generative AI.

- **Deep Learning Specialization (DeepLearning.AI):** Advanced certification for AI engineers.

Additional Resources

Books:

- "Hands-On Machine Learning with Scikit-Learn, Keras, and TensorFlow" – Aurélien Géron
- "Deep Learning" – Ian Goodfellow, Yoshua Bengio and Aaron Courville
- "The Hundred-Page Machine Learning Book" – Andriy Burkov

Tools and Libraries:

- TensorFlow, PyTorch, Scikit-Learn
- OpenAI API, Hugging Face, Google Vertex AI
- Jupyter Notebook, Google Colab

Communities and Forums:

- Kaggle (AI Competition and Learning)
- Stack Overflow (Technical Questions)
- AI Alignment Forum (Discussions on safety and ethics in AI)

Career opportunities

Professionals with expertise in AI are increasingly in demand for a variety of roles, from data analysis to advanced model development. Below, we highlight some of the top career opportunities in AI.

Data Scientist

Responsible for collecting, processing and analyzing large volumes of data, using machine learning techniques to extract valuable insights for companies.

Required Skills:

- Programming in Python or R
- Statistics and applied mathematics
- Machine Learning and Deep Learning
- Big Data Manipulation (Hadoop, Spark)

Machine Learning Engineer

Focuses on developing, training, and deploying machine learning models in production environments.

Required Skills:

- Knowledge of frameworks such as TensorFlow and PyTorch
- Software engineering and good development practices
- MLOps for model scalability

AI Engineer

Works on creating intelligent solutions, developing algorithms for computer vision, NLP (Natural Language Processing) and reinforcement learning.

Required Skills:

- Modeling AI algorithms
- Knowledge of neural networks and computer graphics
- Applications in robotics and automation

Natural Language Processing (NLP) Specialist

Develops solutions that allow machines to understand and generate human language, such as chatbots and virtual assistants.

Required Skills:

- Natural Language Modeling
- Using transformers and LLMs (Large Language Models)
- APIs and libraries like Hugging Face and spaCy

AI Ethics and Regulatory Analyst

Ensures that AI systems are developed ethically, responsibly and within current regulations.

Required Skills:

- Knowledge of data privacy and security
- Principles of ethical AI
- Regulations such as GDPR and LGPD

AI Solutions Architect

Designs scalable infrastructures for implementing AI systems by integrating cloud services and performance optimization.

Required Skills:

- Software architecture
- Cloud computing (AWS, Azure, Google Cloud)
- Databases and data pipelines

Studies and Real Cases of Artificial Intelligence Use

Introduction

Artificial Intelligence (AI) has been widely adopted by companies across different sectors to optimize processes, improve customer experience, and increase operational efficiency. However, its implementation can also present challenges and failures when not used correctly. In this study, we explore success and failure cases in the use of AI, extracting valuable lessons for future applications.

Success Stories in AI Implementation

Amazon – Recommendation Algorithms

Amazon uses AI to personalize product recommendations, resulting in a significant increase in sales. Its algorithms analyze customers' purchase and browsing history to provide accurate suggestions, making the user experience more efficient.

Lessons Learned:

- AI-based personalization can increase customer retention.
- The use of Big Data and Machine Learning improves the accuracy of recommendations.

Tesla – Autonomous Driving

Tesla has revolutionized the automotive industry with its self-driving technology. Using advanced neural networks and deep learning, its vehicles can identify objects, predict behaviors, and improve road safety.

Lessons Learned:

- AI applied to the automotive sector can reduce accidents and improve urban mobility.
- Continuous learning of models improves the efficiency of autonomous systems.

Google – Artificial Intelligence in Google Search

Google has implemented AI into its search engine to better understand user intent and provide more relevant results. BERT (Bidirectional Encoder Representations from Transformers) has helped improve the interpretation of complex queries.

Lessons Learned:

- AI can make search engines more intuitive and efficient.
- NLP (Natural Language Processing) based models improve context understanding.

Netflix – AI for Content Recommendations

Netflix uses AI to recommend movies and TV shows based on user preferences. Its predictive model improves the user experience and helps reduce the subscription cancellation rate.

Lessons Learned:

- Analyzing behavior patterns can predict preferences with high accuracy.
- AI improves user experience by providing personalized suggestions.

AI Implementation Failure Cases

Microsoft – Chatbot Tay

In 2016, Microsoft launched the Tay chatbot on Twitter, designed to learn from human interactions. However, it quickly began generating offensive comments and was shut down within 24 hours.

Lessons Learned:

- AI learning must be supervised to avoid bias and inappropriate behavior.
- NLP models need robust filters to avoid offensive responses.

Amazon – AI-Powered Recruitment System

Amazon developed an AI-based recruiting system, but found that it discriminated against female candidates in favor of male candidates. The project has been discontinued.

Lessons Learned:

- AI models need to be audited to avoid built-in biases.
- Transparency in AI development is essential to ensure fairness.

Apple – Apple Card Credit Algorithm

The Apple Card has been criticized for offering significantly lower credit limits to women than men, raising concerns about algorithmic bias.

Lessons Learned:

- AI applied to financial decisions should be tested to eliminate gender or racial bias.
- It is essential to constantly review models to ensure fairness and equity.

Uber – Autonomous Car and the Fatal Accident

Uber's self-driving car project suffered a major setback when one of its cars hit a pedestrian in 2018. The AI failed to correctly recognize the obstacle.

Lessons Learned:

- AI systems must undergo rigorous testing before operating in critical environments.
- Human supervision remains essential to ensure safety.

Conclusion

Artificial Intelligence has the potential to transform entire businesses and industries, bringing efficiency and innovation. However, its implementation requires care to avoid problems such as algorithmic bias, lack of oversight, and security risks. Lessons learned from successes and failures serve as valuable guides for future AI applications.